Meandering Down The Highway

A Year On The Road With Fulltime RVers

Nick Russell

Publishing Partners
Boulder City, Nevada

Copyright © 2001 by Publishing Partners
ISBN 0-9712491-11-3

All rights reserved. No portion of this publication may be reproduced, stored in a retrieval system, or transmitted in any form or by any means, including electronic, mechanical, photocopying, recording or otherwise, without the prior written permission of the publisher, except for brief quotations for the purpose of review.

Published by Publishing Partners
1400 Colorado Street, Suite C-16
Boulder City, Nevada 89005

Printed in the United States of America

To my co-pilot, navigator, best friend, wife, and partner in business and life, Miss Terry

Meander - aimless wandering; rambling; to wander aimlessly or idly.

Contents

And So We Hit The Road..........................Page 1

Chapter 1   July-August, 1999............................Page 5
Road Trip - Cruising Down The Mother Road - Weekend In Tucson - Final Steps

Chapter 2   September-October, 1999.....................Page 31
On The Road At Last - Adventures In Cowboy Country - Scenic Byways And Wild Rivers - Back To School - Destination: Oregon Coast - Cheese, Classic Aircraft, Crabs And Clams - Wandering Through Washington

Chapter 3   November-December, 1999....................Page 73
Back To The Coast - Breakdown - On To California - Fun On The Beach - Moving On - Back Home In Arizona - Fleetwood Flops - RV Shopping - Desert Nomads

Chapter 4   January-February, 2000......................Page 107
On The Road Again - We Visit A Real Ghost Town - Into The Lone Star State - The Shrine Of Texas Liberty - Texas Nomads - Making New Friends - South Of Houston - Of Prisons And Escapees - Update On The RV From Hell - Wonderful Waco - Christmas Cheer - Closing Out The Twentieth Century

Chapter 5   March-April, 2000............................Page 137
Louisiana Backroads, Southern Sights, Mansions And Beaches - Getting To Know New Orleans - Moving On - Winter Storm -

Oil, Wind And Cattle - Retracing Earlier Routes - The Motorhome From Hell Goes Back To The Factory

Chapter 6 **May-June, 2000..................................Page 163**
Radio Radicals - Off The Road And Homeless - I've Got A Greyhound Feeling - Our First Escapade - Moving On - Some Days Are Diamonds, Some Days Are Stones - Utah Is Ugly - Zion National Park - Rocky Mountains - Very Bad Weather

Chapter 7 **July-August, 2000..............................Page 189**
Getting To Know Colorado - Albuquerque Adventures - Into The Oven - A Tucson Stop - Land Of Enchantment - Music Stars, Free Campgrounds, And The World's Tallest Windmill - Oklahoma Is OK - Winding Our Way Through The Ozarks - Big Fun In Branson - The Secret That Is Missouri - Mark Twain Country

Epilogue..Page 215

Meandering Down The Highway

And So We Hit The Road

We were no different than so many other baby boomer couples - overworked, stressed out to the breaking point, and wanting to make a change. Between the pressures of running two businesses, the long hours required to make the climb up the ladder to "success" and the demands on our time from every direction, we never seemed to have the time to stop and smell the roses. Heck, we usually didn't even have the time to just sit down and talk about where we were, how we got there and where we were going from there.

Sure, we had all of the toys that come with success - a nice home, complete with redwood deck and sunken hot tub, a minivan and four wheel drive pickup, and even four classic cars in our huge new custom-built garage. But at the end of one exhausting day we looked at each other over the kitchen table and asked ourselves "why?" Why have a Corvette, if we never had the time to drive it? Why have this big house when it was just the two of us and the kids were grown up and on their own? Why work 70 or 80 hours a week or more? Did we really want to do this forever? What fun was it going to be even if we did end up being the richest people in the graveyard?

Miss Terry and I have always loved to travel. As an Air Force brat, she spent her formative years moving from duty station to duty station. My father's work uprooted our family so many times in our childhood that I really had no emotional ties to any place I called "home." We both seemed to have a bit of gypsy in our souls. Our dream was to someday buy a motorhome and take to the road. But, at age 46 and with one heart attack under my belt already, one has to wonder just how good the chances of making

Meandering Down The Highway

it to "someday" really are.

So, late in 1998 we found ourselves standing on an RV dealer's lot in Mesa, Arizona, and within days we were the proud owners of a Pace Arrow Vision 36 foot motorhome, complete with all the goodies, including two slideout rooms, an on-board washer/dryer combination, a side by side refrigerator/freezer and a satellite TV dish on the roof. All the comforts of home, even if it lacked the square footage of our "real" home. But, we had realized that even with all the floor space in our current home, we actually utilized very little of it - a great majority of our time was spent seated at the kitchen table eating or reading, parked in front of my computer or sleeping in our bed. The rest of the space in our home was filled with "stuff" - stuff we seldom used: a huge collection of antiques, two bedrooms that had gone unused since the last child became an adult, closets full of clothing we no longer wore. Among its other amenities, our new motorhome had a kitchen table, a bed, and we added a computer workstation - plenty of room to accommodate the activities we enjoyed during our few free hours a week. And because it was so much smaller than our house, a lot of that "stuff" we had been hanging on to would have to go. Suddenly, downsizing and taking to the open road was very appealing to us.

There were a lot of things to consider when making such a major lifestyle change. What about our many friends we would be leaving behind? What about all of the work we had put into arriving at the station in life we presently occupied? What about our beautiful home, filled with all of our "stuff?" Someone asked if we were really willing to give all of that up to run off in a motorhome and travel all around the country, stopping in a new place every few days or weeks, being surrounded by strangers, and relinquishing the "security" our conventional lifestyle held? We looked at each other, grinned and said "YES!"

And so we hit the road. We've both been workaholics for so

Meandering Down The Highway

long that we knew we couldn't live life as an endless vacation, nor would our budget allow it. We knew there were many people who traveled full time and earned some or all of their money as they went. Miss Terry and I sat down, listed all of our talents and skills and discussed how those abilities might be able to help us earn a living as we traveled around the country.

I've owned several small businesses, and had spent years as the editor and publisher of small town community newspapers. We were confident my experience in crunching words, advertising, and newspaper production could be put to use somewhere - hence the *Gypsy Journal*.

As a lifelong gun collector, I was familiar with the gun show scene and knew quite a few people who made good money displaying and selling at gun shows. We were both avid flea market shoppers, always searching for an antique oil lamp or other goodies that caught our eye and would fit into our collection. Over the years we had met and talked with many people who picked up spare change, or even made a fulltime business out of flea market vending. Miss Terry's good eye for a bargain and sharp negotiating skills could very well make flea market vending a profitable addition to our income earning plans.

As the working manager of a commercial glass shop, my wife had put many a good old boy in his place when "that little gal" climbed up onto the hood of his eighteen-wheeler to repair a rock chip before it spread into a spider web of cracks, or even replaced the giant windshield herself. The equipment and materials needed to repair windshields were small and fit easily into one of the basement storage bins of our motor home. Another income possibility.

We realized that, if nothing else, we both possessed strong work ethics and a willingness to do whatever it takes to get any job done. We had managed and owned businesses long enough to know that those are qualities most employers in this country are

Meandering Down The Highway

always seeking, and decided that somehow or someway, yes we could make a buck when we needed to.

The *Gypsy Journal* is our record of our travels. We'll share with you the places we go, the people we meet and the things we see. As we learn more about the full timers' lifestyle, we'll report on our discoveries. When we find some neat little out of the way town that interests us, we'll share it with you. And maybe some day another overworked couple out there will look at each other over the kitchen table at the end of a long, stressful day and say to themselves "If they can do it, we can too!" When that day arrives, we hope our experiences will help you make the decision to escape to the freedom you so very much deserve. If you encounter us along the road somewhere, honk and wave as you pass.

Meandering Down The Highway

July-August, 1999

In future editions, this column will be a travelogue of our journeys. Since this first issue of *the Gypsy Journal* was written before we left on our great adventure, this first *Meandering* column will take in two or three short trips, and the preparations made prior to taking to the road permanently.

When we made the decision to become fulltimers, our first big task was to dispose of most of our worldly possessions. When Miss Terry and I married, just over a year before, we combined our two three bedroom households into one, and every closet, corner and spare room was packed. For two who claim not to have much interest in material possessions, we sure had managed to accumulate a great number over the years.

Since our plans did not call for settling down into a conventional home anytime in the foreseeable future, and because the cost of storage would have been out of our reach, yard sales became a part of the preparations for our new lifestyle.

Some things we learned after holding several yard sales: Your newspaper advertisement can say "Sale starts at 8 a.m. *No Early Birds"* in big bold letters, but plan on being awakened anytime after 5:30 a.m. by eager beavers who just know you'll let them in early; If you think it's junk and are almost embarrassed to put it out in your sale, don't haul it to the dump! It will be the first thing that sells. Among the items that were gobbled up by eager shoppers were several used straw hats, coffee mugs, broken tools, and two lifetime supplies of miscellaneous "junk" we had originally consigned to the trash pile. There are dedicated yard sale shoppers who will not be deterred by rain, snow or hurricane

Meandering Down The Highway

force winds - if you advertise a sale and Mother Nature decides to throw a tantrum the same day, you had better plan on being open for business. Your customers will be there waiting when you crawl out of bed. And if it takes two or three or four or more sales to dispose of everything, you'll see many of the same faces at every sale. Yard sale fanatics are a die hard bunch. Don't forget that your original purpose in holding a yard sale is to dispose of things. Be flexible in your pricing. You don't have to give things away, but shoppers expect a bargain. We were surprised by how much money we took in from our sales, money that will come in very handy on the road.

There are bound to be some things you just can't stand to part with. This is when you have to decide if they are worth paying to store, if you can impose on a friend or relative to stash them for you, or if there is any way they will fit into your RV. When it gets down to the wire, except for treasured family photos and certain mementoes, we were surprised how easy it was to let most things go. Of course, there were certain possessions that really tugged at our heart strings - a few pieces from Miss Terry's huge collection of antique oil lamps, and my much beloved 1969 Corvette, a car I had lusted after ever since high school, and took nearly 30 years to possess. But we forced ourselves to become ruthless and concentrated on what adventures awaited us down the road.

We had purchased a new 1999 Toyota Tacoma four wheel drive pickup to serve as a dinghy. We shopped several dealers before making our purchase at Big Two Toyota in Mesa, Arizona. Big Two, and our salesman, Steve Kuhn, went out of their way to make our purchase a pleasant experience, without any of the game playing and high pressure that so many automobile dealerships seem to thrive on. We had previously seen another Toyota pickup, equipped exactly the same as the one we bought, at Superstition Springs Toyota in Mesa. We were turned off, however, when the salesman wouldn't even show us a vehicle

Meandering Down The Highway

until he had run a credit check to "qualify" us for the price range. By the time he finished fiddling with his computer and satisfied himself that we were indeed buyers, with very good credit, we had already decided to look elsewhere and another salesman spent the commission he could have.

    This tendency for salespeople to worry more about whether or not a potential customer has the ability to buy than in demonstrating their products has always been a pet peeve of mine. Last winter, when we made the decision to go fulltime, we started our shopping at the RV Super Center in Mesa. We arrived on the lot on a Friday evening, a half hour or so before closing time. Aware that there wasn't sufficient time to select an RV, we at least wanted to make contact and perhaps to pick up some brochures to peruse overnight so we'd at least have some idea of a unit that might meet our needs, and make an appointment to come back the next morning. We arrived on the lot dressed in the comfortable jeans and sweatshirts we had worn on the two hour drive from our home. Apparently we didn't look old enough or wealthy enough to attract a salesman's interest - several stood on the patio and watched us peering in the windows of several Class A units, but no one approached us to offer assistance. We finally walked up to the salesmen and told them we were in the market for a motorhome. One salesman reluctantly detached himself from the group and led us inside to his office, where he quickly turned us over to another salesman, who told us *if* we could scrape up $10,000 and come back the next day, he had a ten year old Class C that might suit our needs. The next day we bought a 1998 Pace Arrow Vision 36 foot motorhome from another dealer in the same city. I've always felt that since I work so hard for my money, anyone who wants to get it from me should be willing to do a little bit of work too.

    Our next stop was Camping World in Mesa, where we had the service department install our tow bar, base plate and do all of

Meandering Down The Highway

the electrical work to set us up for safe towing. We also had them install a Rock Solid protective guard to protect the dinghy. Camping World also installed our Banks Power Pak and we've been very happy with their service department and the friendliness of their personnel. Jim, the service writer, and Kelly, the mechanic, are great guys and really went out of their way to help us. We chose to go with the Roadmaster Falcon 5250 tow bar because so many RVers we talked to were pleased with the unit's ease of operation and performance.

Ray Eastburg at Arabian Truck Caps and Accessories, Inc. in Flagstaff, Arizona helped us with the purchase of our SnugTop shell and bed liner. Ray's a great guy, and a lot of fun to do business with. He has a dry sense of humor and will have you laughing from the minute you walk in the door. We were very satisfied with the purchase price and service we received from Ray, and I can recommend him without hesitation. Arabian also has a location in Prescott Valley, Arizona, but if you shop there you won't get the opportunity to have Ray pick on you. It's worth the trip to Flagstaff just for that.

We had to make several trips to the Phoenix area to get our rig ready for the road. Miss Terry's parents have a permanent lot in Carriage Manor in Mesa, and even though it's an over age 55 resort and we're in our mid-40s, my inlaws managed to arrange for special permission for us to park overnight when we were there. Carriage Manor is a beautiful resort, with every amenity, including pool, hobby and craft shops, recreation room and anything else visitors could want. If we met the age requirements, we'd probably spend a fair amount of time at Carriage Manor when we are in the area. Then again, our itchy feet would probably make it hard for us to remain in any one location for too long.

Road Trip

We left our home in Show Low, Arizona about 2 p.m. on

Meandering Down The Highway

Friday, May 7th for our first real trip in the motorhome. Miss Terry drove the RV, while I followed along behind in the Toyota pickup. This was Terry's first solo drive in the big rig, but she handled it like she's been RVing all her life. My pretty lady has never been one to fall back on her considerable feminine charms to avoid anything - she's always right in there doing whatever needs done.

Driving through the Salt River Canyon, that awesome and sometimes intimidating miniature Grand Canyon bisected by U.S. Highway 60, Terry handled the sharp curves and steep downhill grades like a pro. We had purchased a pair of 14 channel Two Way Family Radios from Radio Shack for truck-to-RV communications and found they worked great, even in the mountains. Much better than a pair of handheld CBs we had experimented with.

We stopped in Globe for a quick meal at Wendy's and rolled into Mesa about 6 p.m. We planned to spend the night in Camping World's parking lot so we'd be there first thing Saturday morning to get the tow bar installed. On the way in, we parked the RV in a church parking lot for a couple of hours and drove the pickup to Terry's parents place. Summer is most definitely on the way, it was very hot. The mountains average about 20 degrees cooler, so we really felt the difference.

Overnighting at Camping World was our first experience dry camping, and getting along on just battery power proved to be a snap. We had filled our fresh water holding tank before we left home, and enjoyed hot showers right there in our home on wheels.

When we pulled into Camping World's parking lot, there were already a couple of other rigs present, including a big fifth wheel and a smaller travel trailer. The only real problem we experienced was a lot of noise all night long from traffic on the nearby Superstition Freeway. Actually, I'm the only one who had

Meandering Down The Highway

a problem with it. I'm convinced Miss Terry could sleep through a tornado. I, on the other hand, tend to be a light sleeper. The worst of it all was the clown who pulled up next to us about 4 a.m. in a diesel pickup and let the noisy thing idle for about fifteen minutes, before he roared off. I had just slipped back into dreamland when he returned and let his engine idle for another quarter hour or so before leaving again. What ever happened to courtesy?

Saturday morning we crawled out of bed about 7 a.m. and fired up the generator to make coffee. There was another Pace Arrow Vision in the parking lot and I struck up a conversation with the owner, Bob Brownrigg of Sun City West. We compared notes on our rigs and Bob told me he had purchased his from Biddulph RV and said they were excellent to do business with. Bob reports that any time he's needed any type of service work, the dealer has gone out of his way to be accommodating. We like to hear that, after some of the horror stories other RV owners have shared with us.

When we dropped the RV off, Jim at Camping World's service desk had told us to expect it to be there all day, so we were pleasantly surprised when we checked in just after noon to find that all of the work was finished and we were ready to roll.

I love Camping World. It's a toy store for RVers, and we always spend much more than we intend to when we visit. We can stop for a box of toilet chemical and walk out with solar windshield covers, clip on book lights and guidebooks to camping for free in Outer Mongolia. And still forget the darn toilet chemical! Oh well, now we have an excuse to go back.

Okay, I need everyone's help here. I keep telling Miss Terry we really need one of those maps for the side of the RV. You know the kind I mean, the ones where you fill in all of the states as you visit them. It's a rolling log of our travels. Miss Terry, being a classy lady and all, relegates them into the same category with those little plastic monkeys and chili peppers that light up

Meandering Down The Highway

and hang from the awning. Her word for such merchandise is tacky. But I think if everyone joins me in a letter writing campaign, she just may give in to the pressure. So help me out here, will you? Let's get the "Let's Get Nick A Map" campaign off and rolling. I really want that map.

Leaving Camping World, my father-in-law, Pete Weber, led us to our overnight parking spot, Terry's grandmother's house. It was my first experience towing the pickup behind the RV, so I guess Pete thought he'd get me broken in right - first he led me onto the freeway, then down a surface street through a construction zone where the barricades and caution signs made for some really tight squeezes. Pete has been a fulltimer for years now, and I suspect he just figured everyone is as confident and skilled behind the wheel as he is. Wrong! I definitely had some white knuckles before we got to our destination. Since we hope to drive to Alaska this summer or next, maybe Pete thought this would be a good test of our skills or something. The dinghy tracks beautifully behind the RV, and you really can't tell it's there on the flats. We would learn, in the next few days, that it does make a difference when driving in the mountains. We had invited Terry's parents out to dinner, and I had been wanting to try the Outback Steakhouse, since I've heard so many good reports on their food and service, but we arrived to find a crowd waiting outside, and were told to expect a two hour wait. It was too hot and we were too hungry to hang around that long, so we headed over to Red Lobster, where we were told the wait would be an hour. It seems that we had chosen prom night to go out to dinner, and every restaurant was full of pretty young girls in formals and their nervous beaus. The wait actually dragged out to about 90 minutes before we finally were seated, and by then we were all starving. One good thing about Red Lobster, among many, is that it's really hard to walk away hungry after a meal. The food is always delicious and we all stuffed ourselves. It was worth the wait.

Meandering Down The Highway

We spent Saturday and Sunday nights parked in the driveway of Terry's grandmother's house in Gilbert. The family matriarch passed away a few months ago, and it was strange to see the house empty. We plugged into electricity and were able to run the air conditioning and watch some television, though the picture quality was poor. Terry and I were both surprised to see how far our water supply was stretching.

Sunday morning, it was strange not to have a thick Sunday newspaper to browse through. Terry got her Juiceman out and whipped up huge glasses of fresh orange juice to go with breakfast. The day started off with a cool breeze, but warmed up later on. It being Mother's Day, we spent the day with Terry's parents. I had managed to come down with some sort of allergy, and spent a good portion of the next few days sniffling and sneezing. Springtime in the desert is a beautiful time of year, with everything in bloom. But all of that pollen sure has an effect on a lot of people. I know Kleenex stock went up about three points just due to my consumption.

Monday morning our supply of fresh water ran out - right in the middle of Terry's shower! I wasted no time in getting out our hoses and hooking up to a faucet to fill our holding tank, while my bride stood soapy and impatient in the RV's shower waiting on me to get done.

Finally rinsed off and calmed down, Miss Terry toasted English muffins for breakfast, then we unhooked the electric cord, retracted the jacks, pulled in the slideouts, and hit the road. We stopped at Circuit City and purchased a Toshiba 2545CDS notebook computer. Though I plan on installing my big Compaq Presario desktop with its 17" screen in the RV for most of my work, the notebook will be necessary for e-mail connections on the road. We also bought a digital telephone and signed up for AT&T's One Rate nationwide service. Not having to pay long distance charges as we travel is going to save us a fortune.

Meandering Down The Highway

We drove up Interstate 17 through central Phoenix and exited onto State Highway 74, headed west. We rolled into Wickenburg and stopped for gas, then at a Bashas grocery store to stock up on a few things. Leaving the shopping center, I made a wrong turn and found myself headed back in the direction we had just come from. But we circled the block and got back on track with a minimum of effort. Wickenburg is a cowboy town, home to several dude ranches, the Desert Caballeros Western Museum, featuring some of the best displays of western history and art anywhere, (including works by Frederick Remington and Charles Russell), and the Hassayampa River Preserve, known nationwide for the many species of birds, reptiles and mammals who live in this lush oasis. The architecture is a blend of Old West and 1950s America.

Like so many places in the modern West, Wickenburg is facing changes. Over the last five years or so, there has been an influx of retirees lured by the clean air, climate and small town atmosphere - so many that old timers fear the very character of the town they hold so dear may soon disappear. For those wanting to keep things as they were, the future looks grim - *Retirement Places Rated* just named Wickenburg to the list of the top five places to retire nationally and the town has been flooded with phone calls and inquiries. Over 60 percent of Wickenburg's population is of retirement age, and locals know it's only a matter of time before Phoenix retirement centers such as Sun City and Sun City West grow to the borders of their town. Somehow the vision of retirees zipping around town in golf carts doesn't sit well with the pickup truck driving Wickenburg image. The town even has new pink sidewalks! What's a cowboy to do?

We arrived at Escapees North Ranch about 3 p.m. and got our first official Escapees hugs from Judy Piper, part of the management team, along with her husband Larry. We're new Escapees members, and this was our first visit to one of their RV parks. Everything I've read about the Escapees organization

Meandering Down The Highway

stresses just how friendly everyone is, and we found it to be very true. Everyone at North Ranch, campers and staff alike, made us feel welcome and a part of the family.

North Ranch is in a pretty setting. Our overnight space was on a level dirt lot with full hookups and a beautiful view across the valley to the Bradshaw Mountains. We got the rig set up in record time, then wandered over to the clubhouse for social hour and a chance to get to know some of our fellow Escapees. Everyone went out of their way to make us feel welcome and we all exchanged bits of information and tips on the RV lifestyle. Since Terry and I are younger than most fulltimers, we were a bit apprehensive about what kind of reception we'd get. Two minutes after parking at North Ranch, all of our concerns dissolved. Everyone we talked to congratulated us on our decision to become fulltimers, and many older RVers told us they wish they hadn't waited so long to hit the road.

Back at our rig, we set up a couple of lawn chairs under the awning, and armed with cold drinks and good books, really began to relax. I can see already I'm really going to enjoy this laid back lifestyle. A cool breeze was blowing gently and I was about as unstressed as I've felt in years.

Our neighbors were in a fifth wheel, and had been at North Ranch several days. They called us over to see a bird's nest, complete with delicate blue egg, that a bird had constructed on the ladder on the rear of their trailer. We didn't get their names, and they set out to return home to Oregon the next morning.

I had not been able to get very good television reception with the RV's antenna, even in Phoenix. But at North Ranch I discovered an antenna booster switch in one of the compartments above the windshield and flipped it on. Voila, we had a clear picture! It's amazing what you can learn as you go. We still haven't been able to get the television to work in the bedroom. It doesn't seem to have any power and we can't figure out why.

Meandering Down The Highway

Monday night we slept soundly and woke up about 7:30 a.m. Tuesday to the sounds of our neighbors hooking up to pull out. I dressed in shorts and a T-shirt and wandered around the park taking pictures while Miss Terry made breakfast. The weather was perfect, much more comfortable than in Phoenix. One more example of the friendliness of other RVers, we were having trouble figuring out how to roll up our big awning when we were breaking camp. A neighboring Escapee saw our dilemma and quickly stepped in to help. In just a minute or two he had talked us through the procedure, and then wished us safe travels as we drove away.

Our stay at North Ranch came to just over $9, not bad at all for full hookups. Escapees is definitely a good investment, especially considering their mail forwarding service and all of the other benefits they provide members.

Judy and Larry told us as we were checking out that they will be heading to the Escapees park in Tennessee to work for the summer, and we hope to meet up with them somewhere in our travels. When Terry mentioned that we have made the decision to go fulltime, Larry told her that there are at least a million Americans living the fulltime lifestyle. "So I guess that makes you one in a million," Larry joked. Shucks, I could have told him that. I've always known my pretty lady was at least one in a million!

We pulled out of North Ranch about 9:30 a.m. and headed toward Prescott. A couple of miles down the road we stopped for an equipment check and discovered that we hadn't unlocked the ignition on the pickup after hooking it behind the RV. Everything seemed to be okay, and no harm was apparently done, but it did remind us of the importance of using a checklist when breaking camp.

Shades of the Bates Hotel - driving through Congress, we spotted a sign advertising rooms for rent and taxidermy services!

Meandering Down The Highway

No thanks, our home on wheels is very comfortable, we'll just sleep here.

The climb up Yarnell Hill was slow, and this is when it became evident that towing an extra 3500 pounds of pickup truck definitely has an impact on the RV's performance. But traffic was light and we sat back to enjoy the ride and the morning. Just outside of Congress Terry spotted a large rock formation that looked like a frog, and someone had painted it to match. Definitely worth a stop for a photo.

Signs advise not taking a big rig over Highway 89 into Prescott, so we turned at Kirkland Junction and went up through Skull Valley on a winding two lane road through some pretty country.

There was a lot of construction going on in Prescott, and Whiskey Row was closed to traffic. We managed to detour around and get to the Safeway grocery on White Spar Road, where the nice folks allowed us to leave the RV so we could go exploring in the pickup.

I've always loved Prescott's beautiful Victorian houses and the shady courthouse square, with it's huge old trees and statues. There's an interesting time line etched into the concrete sidewalk flanking the main entrance to the courthouse, reporting on events in the area from the earliest days to the present. It's fun to spend a little bit of time learning about the history of the area you're visiting. I guess that's why I never can pass one of those historical markers I spot along the highways and byways we travel.

We browsed through some of the neat antique shops in the downtown area and had a pizza at Tastebuds Pizza on Cortez Street. The food was good, but I think the manager was having a bad day, we never did see him smile. The restaurant has an art gallery upstairs, with several nice paintings on display.

After our meal, we drove out through the Granite Dells, an area of interesting rock formations, and past Watson Lake and

Meandering Down The Highway

Embry Riddle Aeronautical University. I'm amazed how much the city has grown over the years. We left Prescott about 5 p.m. and experienced some really heavy traffic going through Prescott Valley. This area was empty prairie only a few years ago, but now is full of strip malls, a Costco, and a horde of impatient drivers rushing to get someplace. It felt more like being in Phoenix or Mesa than in the small town I remembered from visits over the years.

We drove to Camp Verde and stopped for the night at the Zane Grey RV Park and immediately fell in love with the place. Zane Grey is a small park, but well laid out and very clean. Every space is raked gravel, all spaces are divided by split rail fences, and most have picnic tables. The park is nicely landscaped and level, with big shady trees. We got a pull-through spot and set up housekeeping. Shirley and Charlie Nelson share the management duties with Carol and Forrest Cole, and everyone is friendly and easygoing. We liked Zane Grey so much we immediately decided to stay an extra day and make it our base camp while we explored the area.

Our rig came with a washer/dryer combination, and Miss Terry decided to give it a try while we were at Zane Grey. Once we realized that we had to flip the switch between the microwave and washing machine, it worked great and she managed to do two or three loads of laundry.

Though Zane Grey sits right alongside Highway 260 and there is some traffic noise, the park's natural setting seems to act as a buffer and we had no trouble sleeping at all. Every day was comfortable, and the nights just cool enough to make snuggling an extra pleasure.

Wednesday morning we left the RV at Zane Grey and drove to Montezuma Castle National Monument, just a few miles north of Camp Verde. Built in the 12th century, this massive five-story cliff dwelling was home to Sinagua Indians, who carved out a

Meandering Down The Highway

home from the steep cliff face alongside Beaver Creek, only to disappear centuries later for reasons still unknown today.

The site is a popular attraction and there were several tour buses loading and unloading while we toured the monument. I heard Japanese, German and French spoken as we passed by various crowds of camera-clicking tourists. I couldn't help but look up at the old ruins high on the face of the cliff and wonder what the ghosts of those ancients must think as they look down on all this activity in their once quiet little valley.

Leaving Montezuma Castle, we drove north on Interstate 17 to State Highway 179, where we turned west to Sedona. Sitting among a magnificent backdrop of massive red rock formations, Sedona is definitely scenic. But it's much too ritzy for my tastes. I'm a meat and potatoes man, and I get uncomfortable in an atmosphere of lattes and designer clothing worn by yuppies and New Agers. To say that Sedona is elitist is an understatement - McDonald's wasn't allowed to use their traditional golden arches on their Sedona restaurant. I guess the City Council thought they were too crass for a special place like Sedona. Instead, the Sedona McDonald's sports small teal green arches on it's signs, in keeping with the community's flavor. Hey folks, it's a burger joint, okay? Just give me my daily dose of cholesterol and let me get back on the road, will ya?

The downtown area of Sedona is a strip of shops offering everything from crystals and incense to expensive jewelry and artworks. We did stop at the Sedona Fudge Company, where I stocked up on several varieties of their Mackinac Island style fudge to keep my sweet tooth happy. I finally gave up on Sedona after browsing through a shop that's signs advertised only the finest quality leather, silver and Native American jewelry. I admired a nice leather belt and almost bought it, until I spotted the words Made in China stamped on the inside. I resent paying premium prices for imported junk, no matter how pretty the

Meandering Down The Highway

community is. That was about the same time that Miss Terry was looking at some spices in a shop - spices that she can buy at home for $5 for three bottles were going for $5.99 each in Sedona. Go for the view, but leave your checkbook in your RV.

From Sedona we drove to the once ghost town of Jerome. Now, Jerome is my kind of town! The shopkeepers are all friendly, it has a laid back feel to it, and you can feel the history emanating from the old buildings around you. Jerome started out as a mining town, and between 1876 and 1938, over a billion dollars worth of copper was hauled out of her mines. But like so many boom towns of the west, Jerome began to die during the Depression. Work went on until 1953, but by then Jerome was nearly deserted. It looked like the place was going to become a ghost town, but a few diehards hung on and eventually the town began to come back to life. Today, about 500 people live in Jerome and it's a popular spot for tourists and bargain hunters who prowl the shops perched on it's steep hillsides in search of art, antiques and other treasures. A word of caution here, if you visit Jerome, leave your RV in Cottonwood or Prescott and drive your dinghy. The winding mountain road is not built for today's big rigs.

Back at Zane Grey, we settled down under our awning and in no time at all I fell asleep in my lawn chair! After years of stress and being on the go all the time, this slower pace is really great. I woke up to the sound of another RV pulling into the space next to ours, a Class C rental unit occupied by an attractive young couple from Switzerland, who are touring the country with their two little girls. The husband was amazed at the size of our wide body rig and told us it would be impossible to drive such an RV on Europe's narrow roads.

An hour or so later, I had gone inside to use the bathroom, and when I came out, Miss Terry told me that our foreign neighbors must not realize just how close the quarters are in an RV park - the

Meandering Down The Highway

pretty blonde woman had stripped down to get ready for bed standing right in front of the window, without closing the blinds. And I missed it! Terry came inside to spare herself and our neighbors any further embarrassment, but I sat outside another two hours swatting bugs, and all I ever got to see was the guy in his boxer shorts! Timing is everything.

Thursday morning we reluctantly rolled up our awnings and pulled out of Zane Grey, heading west on Highway 260. The climb up into the high country was slow at times, but the road winds through some gorgeous country and there are plenty of pullouts to let traffic pass.

We rolled through the rustic little communities of Strawberry and Pine, then pulled into Tonto Natural Bridge State Park. If there was an earlier warning sign, I never saw it, so we were on top of the downhill road into the park before we spotted a marker telling us a two mile long 14% grade lay ahead. I put the transmission in low and gave the brakes an application every now and then on the sharp curves and we made it to the bottom with no problem. The road is steep and curving, but also wide and in good repair. If you go, I'd advise parking your RV outside the park and using your dinghy.

Tonto Natural Bridge is the largest travertine bridge in the world, at 183 feet high and 400 feet long. The park headquarters is located in a lovely historic old lodge, and the entire park sits in a beautiful valley surrounded by pine-covered mountains. We first took the short 300 foot waterfall trail, a steep climb down to a natural grotto that's worth every vertical foot of the trail. Coming back up, we met a group of young school kids scampering along like they had good sense, and we envied them their energy. Pausing to rest at a picnic table after we were back on top, I walked away and left my 35mm Nikon camera behind on the table. When I realized it was gone, I raced back to the spot, expecting the worst, only to find it waiting right where I left it,

Meandering Down The Highway

among the crowd of young people we had passed earlier.

There are three walking tours in the park, and warning signs caution visitors with health problems not to attempt them. Take these warnings seriously, the trails are steep and strenuous. Only attempt them if you are in good physical condition and wearing sturdy footwear. At one point, you'll find yourself hanging onto steel cables as you descend the steep path to the bottom of the canyon.

But the arduous trip is well worth the effort. A stream flows through the tunnel at the bottom of the natural bridge, and it's one of the most beautiful sights you'll ever see. Miss Terry and I clambered over the slippery wet rocks, getting sprayed by the cold water falling from the top, to a spot under the bridge. It was easily 25 degrees cooler, the water, shade and breeze coming up the canyon combining to provide natural air conditioning.

After relaxing under the bridge for a spell, we continued on the trail, stopping along the way to catch our breath and watch fish in the stream. We spent several minutes observing a crow as it frolicked on the air currents at the top of the bridge, dipping into the waterfall, then out to float on the wind, before it plunged down, then back up again. Obviously, the bird was having itself a ball in this natural wonderland.

The climb out of the bottom of the canyon was not quite as steep as going down, and strategically placed benches along the trail give weary climbers a chance to catch their breath and give their twitching leg muscles a break.

Back at the RV, we quenched our thirst, then prepared for that long drive back up the steep road to the highway. Surprisingly, the RV performed like a champ and we made it without much effort.

Back on Highway 260, we passed through Payson, then across the Mogollon Rim through Kohl's Ranch, Christopher Creek, Forest Lakes, Heber-Overgaard, and home to Show Low. The wind had picked up, and the last 35 miles or so was white-

Meandering Down The Highway

knuckle two handed driving as the gusts did their best to throw us across the center line of the highway every minute or so

We could feel all the old tensions coming back with every mile of highway that rolled out behind us as we got closer and closer to home. "I wish we didn't have to go back and wrap so many things up," Terry said. "I just want to turn this thing around and keep on going down the highway." I nodded in agreement, both of us knowing that for us, home was no longer the walls we had lived within back in Show Low. The trip had been the final transformation for us, and now home was the open road and wherever our new RV lifestyle takes us.

Cruising Down The Mother Road

May 26 found us on the road to Kingman, Arizona for a visit with my old friend Mike Howard. We had reservations for two tables at the Memorial Weekend Gun Show at the Mohave County Fairgrounds, and I can never pass up an excuse to get off the interstate and onto old Route 66. The longest remaining stretch of the old highway runs from Seligman, Arizona to the California border at Topock, and is a must for dedicated Route 66 road warriors.

Just outside of Ash Fork, still on Interstate 40, we spotted something amiss with a big fifth wheeler ahead of us. Something seemed to be dragging underneath, so I pulled alongside and motioned the driver to pull over. As it turned out, he had an outboard motor in the back of his pickup, complete with five gallon plastic gasoline can attached by a long hose. The can had blown out of the back of the truck and was merrily bouncing along the roadway under the trailer. We were happy we spotted the problem before something set the fuel ablaze. That can really ruin an RVer's day!

Our first night in Kingman, Mike, Miss Terry and I had dinner at the new Cracker Barrel on Stockton Hill Road. I'd never eaten at a Cracker Barrel before, but I can tell you that I'll be back

Meandering Down The Highway

often. Their portions are huge, the prices are fair, and Denise, our waitress, was friendly and a lot of fun. The only drawback was deciding which of the many delicious menu offerings to choose. Miss Terry and I had the catfish, and it was really good.

Friday afternoon Mike drove us over to visit the Power House, headquarters of the Historic Route 66 Association of Arizona, and we stopped for cheeseburgers at Mr. D'z Diner across the street. The food was okay, I prefer my burgers a trifle more moist, but the root beer was fabulous. While we ate, one of the waitresses entertained us as she stood at the counter telling a friend all the latest gossip about who was seeing who, who was cheating on who, and who was trying (and not succeeding) at quitting smoking. A few minutes of eavesdropping at any small town lunch counter and you can get a pretty good fix on what's going on in town, no matter where you are.

The gun show turned out to be pretty successful for us, and Bernard Murphy, the promoter, treated all of the exhibitors to a steak dinner Saturday afternoon. We plan on getting a table at some of his upcoming shows in Kingman and Yuma.

We hung around town until Tuesday morning to allow all of the holiday travelers to get off the highway, then headed eastbound on Old 66 toward home. I just love the quiet drive through the countryside. New owners have taken over Hackberry, and I had to stop to take a picture of a lovely old Corvette parked outside.

We were tempted to stop for a milkshake at the Snow Cap Drive-in in Seligman and a few minutes of craziness with the owner, but since we had an appointment in Flagstaff, decided to pass this trip. But we can't go through Williams without stopping to visit with my friend Paul Taylor and his pretty wife Sandi at *Route 66 Magazine.* The place was crowded, and Paul has added some new merchandise to their gift shop. They're in the middle of an expansion and will be moving into larger quarters next door

Meandering Down The Highway

once all of the construction work is finished. Paul spent some time traveling in an RV and doing some freelance writing a few years ago, and he offered a tip or two about life on the road. He also kindly offered to put a little news release about the birth of the *Gypsy Journal in* the Fall issue of his magazine, for which we are grateful. We need all of the exposure we can get.

We almost made it out of Williams without stopping at Twisters Soda Fountain for one of their thick chocolate milkshakes, but the darned engine just sort of died right in front of the place and I was lucky to be able to coast to the curb. I guess it was just one of those mysterious mechanical flukes, because after a few minutes of wandering through Twisters' gift shop, our milkshakes were ready and that old engine started right up and purred like a kitten. Go figure.

Route 66 is the main drag in Flagstaff, and was crowded as usual. We stopped to visit with Ray at Arabian Truck Caps, wandered around town a little bit, then got back on Interstate 40 headed toward Show Low. The trip down the super slab went pretty fast after our meandering cruise down old Route 66, and in just over two hours we were back at the old homestead. Ten minutes after we parked, I was already raring to get back on the road. The last few weeks of preparation and taking care of final details just seem to be dragging for us. There's so much waiting just down the road and we want to see all of it right now!

Weekend In Tucson

On a Friday morning in June we pulled out of Show Low and pointed the RV south on Highway 60, headed for the big gun show at the Tucson Convention Center. I was a little apprehensive about the stretch of Highway 77 between Globe and Winkleman, Arizona, because it has some pretty steep hills, but we managed just fine, pulling to the side a time or two to allow the traffic behind us to get past.

We stopped at a roadside park in Mammoth for a quick

Meandering Down The Highway

snack, one of the best benefits of traveling in an RV. Miss Terry had made up a batch of her delicious brownies the night before we left, and I didn't want to offend her by not stuffing myself. A guy has to show his appreciation for the finer things in life, you know.

We arrived at the Prince of Tucson RV Park about 4 p.m. Being the off season, the place wasn't too crowded. The parking spaces are rather narrow, and it took two or three attempts before I got in and straightened out, and by the time we hooked up the power cord and sewer and water hoses, it sure felt good to have those two big air conditioners on the roof of the RV blowing cold air.

After resting up a little bit, Miss Terry and I drove over to the Convention Center to register, then headed out to the big Tanque Verde Swap Meet for some bargain hunting. I lived in Tucson for many years, but it's been nearly a decade since I moved away and the place sure has changed. Where in the world do they find all of that concrete, anyway?

Saturday morning, bright and early, we were back at the Convention Center and setting up our table. It seems that whoever is in charge of planning events for the city wanted to get as much revenue as possible, so while the gun show was held in one portion of the complex there was a huge Watchtower convention going on in another part. It was a nightmare for a guy like me! I respect anybody's religion, but I demand to be left alone to believe in my own way, and I've spent a lifetime telling various missionaries who come to my door that I'm not interested. Now here I was, surrounded by hundreds, maybe thousands, of Jehovah's Witnesses! (If you live in an RV and park in a different place every few days, do they still find their way to your doorstep? Back home it wasn't much of a problem, since Cujo, my agnostic, evil spirited 100 pound German shepherd kept the Witnesses, Mormons and UPS guy at bay, but he won't fit in the RV.)

Meandering Down The Highway

With so much going on in one place, parking was terrible and many exhibitors and customers complained loudly about having to pay $4 to park and then walk so far to get into the gun show. Tucson has never been known for wise planning, though greed is one of their big things. $55 each for vendor tables, $4 a day to park, then the city demands 2% of all vendor sales. Not to mention the unpopular RV parking tax Pima County put in a year or so ago. We won't be attending any more events in the Convention Center.

We did run into a stroke of good luck - our tables were right next to Dorothy Weymouth. Dorothy is a full time RVer who displays at 50 gun shows a year, making a circuit throughout the western United States. She offered us a lot of great tips about merchandising, the show circuit, and life on the road. We're always eager to pick up another tidbit or two of knowledge, and Dorothy is a walking encyclopedia. We learned a lot from her in two days.

Prince of Tucson RV Park is a clean place, and the man who checked us in was friendly, but there were three things that really turned us off. The park is hard beside Interstate 10 and the railroad tracks, so it was pretty noisy. And nearby is some sort of sewage treatment plant, so it got rather smelly at night, making it sort of unpleasant for sitting outside once the sun went down. The thing that really got to me, and if I'm wrong here, somebody please tell me so, is that checkout time was 11 a.m. Sunday and the gun show didn't get over until 5 p.m. When I inquired if we might leave our RV, unhooked of all water and utilities, until after the show, they wanted to charge us $2 an hour.

That added up to another $12, on top of the space rental we had already paid! I might understand that if it was the busy season and space was at a premium, but not when there were empty sites all over the place. Especially not after dropping nearly $50 for two nights already. I've asked for the same courtesy at other RV

Meandering Down The Highway

parks and never been charged. Have I been lucky so far, and is charging by the hour the general rule in such cases, or are these guys getting a little too greedy? Someone please clue me in.

We bought gasoline for $1.06 a gallon before leaving Tucson, the lowest price we've seen in a while. When we left Tucson Sunday afternoon, we debated going back up to the mountains the same way we came in, or by the longer (but flatter) route through Florence, Arizona. We decided to just retrace our path. We learn by our mistakes. By the time we got through Winkleman and reached that narrow, winding section of highway to Globe it was dark. My night vision isn't what it used to be, and it was pretty hard to judge just how much room I had between us and the guardrail a time or two, especially when meeting other big RVs or eighteen wheelers head on. We made it okay, but my nerves were really on edge by the time we pulled into the Star Mart in Globe for a soda and snack. By the time we made it back to Show Low, it was midnight, and that old bed sure looked inviting. We decided after that experience that we won't attempt driving any long distances the same day a show or event ends - after two or three days on our feet, it's just too tiring. Besides, that's why we have our home on wheels. Why drive five or six hours through the night to sleep when we have our bed right there with us, wherever we are?

Final Steps

We finally got everything moved out of the house in Show Low, our real estate agent stuck a sign in the front yard, and on June 13th we moved the RV back down to Terry's grandmother's in Gilbert, Arizona to take care of a few last minute details and put the finishing touches on the *Gypsy Journal* before hitting the road.

We checked out several RV parks in Mesa and Apache Junction for a place to squat for a couple of weeks, and were amazed at the differences in prices and amenities. Some places

Meandering Down The Highway

were pure rat holes, and we didn't even pull in. There's just something about beer bottles in the driveway and broken down automobiles deteriorating in the desert sun that turns me off.

Many of the nicer parks and resorts were off limits to us, since we're not 55 years old. I guess they don't want a bunch of kids running around making noise, but since it's just the two of us and we're more than halfway through our 40s, we felt kind of discriminated against. I hope this won't be an ongoing problem as we travel. Do other baby boomers run into this on the road?

We settled in and quickly remembered why we moved away from the desert so many years ago. Our first full day in Gilbert, the thermometer peaked at 106 degrees and these cool mountain-pampered bodies of ours had a real problem adjusting. We had planned on staying in the Phoenix area through the Fourth of July weekend before hitting the road, but after a week or two in the summer's heat, we're thinking the cool Northwest sure sounds inviting.

The morning after we arrived we got a scare - I had set up my Compaq desktop computer to do some work when smoke began pouring out of the surge suppressor. Quickly shutting off the power and disconnecting everything, I was sure I'd burned up my computer. But it appears the surge suppressor did it's job and sacrificed itself to protect the Compaq, because after checking the outlet power with a voltmeter to be sure everything was okay, I plugged the computer back in and everything seemed to be working fine. Must have been a power surge or something.

The folks in the house next door have a menagerie - chickens, turkeys, assorted other fowl, a steer, and a goat, not to mention assorted dogs, cats and possibly a gerbil or two. I think the animals are more pets than livestock. We got a laugh watching the steer and goat play together. The goat stands on its hind legs and butts the steer between the eyes. The steer doesn't seem to mind this, he just lowers his head and gently butts his smaller friend

Meandering Down The Highway

back, sending the goat sailing. The tenacious goat rights itself and comes right back for more. From time to time the steer seems to give his little buddy an ego boost by rocking backward when the goat rams him. They do this for hours. Who says animals don't have a sense of play?

I know our resident critter does. Let me say right off that I'm not a cat person. I'm too insecure to own a cat. Cats are independent and really don't care if you're there or not except when they want food, water, or fresh kitty litter. I need more than that from a pet. I'm a dog person. Dogs let you know they're glad to see you. Walk outside to check the mail, and your average dog will dislocate his hips wagging his tail in greeting when you return. Venture as far afield as the nearest grocery store and your dog will pee on the carpet in his excitement to see you come home. Dogs are good for my ego, even if they are hard on the carpet.

That said, I live with a cat. When I poured enough vino down Miss Terry's gullet to get her to agree to marry me, she made one stipulation - "Love me, love my cat." The morning after, her eyes may have been bleary, but her conviction was just as clear. So I live with a cat.

But not just any cat, no siree! I must admit, Sasquatch is an amazing feline. A Lynx/Manx/Himalayan mix, this boy weighs in at about thirty pounds, has six or seven toes on each massive foot, and he's been known to send coonhounds whimpering away with their tails tucked safely between their legs. I guess if a guy's got to have a cat, Sasquatch is as close to a good dog as you can get.

Sasquatch knows I'm not a cat person, so he uses every cat trick in the book to get my attention - from plopping himself between me and my book when I'm reading, to reaching out with his claw-filled foot to snag my trouser leg as I pass by. His favorite game is to wait until I'm too deep in slumber to boot him

Meandering Down The Highway

off the foot of the bed, then lay in wait until my dreams find me shipwrecked on a desert island with the likes of Meg Ryan, Heather Locklear, and Brooke Shields. Just as I'm about to announce which lucky lass gets to wander down to the waterfall for an invigorating shower, followed by a dip in the warm waters of the lagoon, Sasquatch brings me back to reality by kneading all sixty or so claws in the bottoms of my feet. I think he's trying to help me set a new record for the broad jump from a prone position, in the fat bald guy category. Yes, I love my cat. Miss Terry says I have to.

Even after all our planning, we still found ourselves wondering where to stash everything in the motorhome. All of those bins, nooks and crannies that looked so huge when the rig was empty sure filled up in a hurry. We are quickly realizing that many of the things we brought along just aren't going to fit, and deciding that we'd rather leave them behind than try to walk around them and have all of our floor space taken up. Miss Terry and I have come to an agreement about sharing precious space that she tells me is mutually equitable - she gets all of the storage inside, underneath, and within a three foot radius of the motorhome. I get the glove compartment of our Toyota pickup all to myself, except for her curling iron and three little egg-shaped panty hose containers, and I have exclusive use of the map pocket in the driver's door. Life is good.

Well, that's it for this issue. We sure hope you enjoyed this first issue of the *Gypsy Journal*. Next issue we'll be reporting back to you on the Life on Wheels Conference and all of the places we wander. Until then, we hope to see you in our travels.

Meandering Down The Highway

September-October, 1999

Whoever said the life of fulltime RVers/newspaper publishers was going to be all fun and games? We left the heat of Arizona's Phoenix valley the end of June and drove north to Flagstaff to get the first *Gypsy Journal* finished and printed. We arrived at Woody Mountain Campground in Flagstaff, set up camp and got to work on pasting up the pages about 3 p.m. on Tuesday, June 29th to meet our printing deadline Wednesday morning.

Well, you know what they say about the best laid plans... whatever could go wrong did go wrong, and it seemed to take forever to get the job done. When we finally added the last correction and laid the last sheet of paper away, the birds were singing and it was daylight! We crawled into bed about 5 a.m. for a couple of hours sleep, and I had just gotten into that comfortable dreamworld of deep sleep when the telephone rang at 8 a.m. Just as well, if I had slept much longer it might have been too late to get to the printer.

Woody Mountain is a nice family park, and the place was packed. Every time we stopped into the office the phones were ringing off the hook and the poor staff was running at full speed trying to take care of their duties, answer questions, and make sure everyone was happy and having a good time. The campground sits right on Route 66, with lots of big trees, a pool, laundry, and other facilities. We look forward to visiting again

Meandering Down The Highway

when we're not so short on time.

I had ordered signs for our pickup's shell from a sign shop in Chandler, Arizona while we were in the Phoenix area, and after finally getting the signs (which were late and way past the deadline they had been promised) they had typos and were the wrong size and type style. We didn't have any more time to wait on a promised redo of the job, and no confidence in the shop's ability at that point, so we canceled the order. While the newspapers were being printed I stopped in at Sign-A-Rama in Flagstaff. After I explained our plight to a really sweet young lady named Lacey Hausladen, she sat down and whipped out the job in no time at all. Lacey's dad, Steve, owns the shop and they really went out of their way to help us, getting the signs done in time for us to be on the road as soon as we picked up the newspapers. Now, that's service! Thanks Lacey and Steve.

On The Road At Last

We were headed to Wyoming for some family time, and wanted to beat the July 4th holiday traffic. We left Flagstaff about 3 p.m. June 30, headed east on Interstate 40. After filling our gas tank at the Flying J in Winslow, we rolled across northern Arizona and into New Mexico. There's an abrupt change in topography when you cross the state line. In that part of the country, Arizona is rather flat, with just a few little mesas and hills. But right at the state line, New Mexico thrusts upward into several huge, red-colored mesas that really catch your eye.

I'm sure there is someplace in this great land of ours where a guy can drive his RV for more than twenty miles without having to go through a construction zone, but I haven't found it yet. Interstate 40 across New Mexico is an obstacle course of rough road, construction zones, and truckers who want to run over you. It's a tribute to Miss Terry's packing abilities that nothing inside the rig was broken as we bounced over potholes, swerved out of the way of psychotic eighteen-wheelers, and rattled through

Meandering Down The Highway

construction zones.

We came through Albuquerque at 9 p.m., turned north on Interstate 25, and things immediately got better. The highway was in good condition, traffic was light, and most of the truckers had stayed on I-40. We were really beginning to feel the effects of our long, sleepless night and the many hours on the highway. About fifteen miles south of Santa Fe, we pulled into the La Bajada Rest Area and took the last spot in the special RV section in back. We ended up parking at a sharp angle, with the foot of our bed pointing downhill, but were just too tired to care. Crawling under the sheets at about 11 p.m., we both went into a coma until 9 the next morning!

If La Bajada is an example of New Mexico rest areas, I think we just might do a majority of our RVing there. The rest area features a special RV section in back, away from the big trucks and highway noise, complete with a dump station. The next morning we picked up a ton of free travel brochures and publications from the nice fellow in the visitor center, and Miss Terry helped herself to a cup of the complimentary coffee. The hills surrounding La Bajada are rich in turquoise, and Indians mined the blue stone and gold in the area long before the first Spanish explorers visited.

I've always wanted to spend some time in Santa Fe, but this trip we were just too short on time, so we stayed on the highway, heading north. We stopped for gas in Las Vegas, New Mexico, and I think I like it a lot more than that other Las Vegas in Nevada, with all the neon lights and crowds. After filling our gas tank we took a quick ride through town. There are lots of neat old gingerbread houses, tree-lined streets that make you think you're driving through a green tunnel, and the people all seemed friendly. I was disappointed that our gas mileage was only about 6.2 miles per gallon, but we're carrying a heavy load, including the newspapers and several boxes of cookbooks that will be

Meandering Down The Highway

delivered to Miss Terry's daughter in Wyoming. I'm sure all the starts and stops in the construction zones didn't help much either.

Northern New Mexico is beautiful, and we promised ourselves a return trip when we have lots of time to explore. The climb up Raton Pass was slow, especially since we got stuck behind two flatbed National Guard trucks hauling heavy equipment, but soon enough we were heading downhill and into Colorado.

That first sight of the Rocky Mountains always takes my breath away. They are truly awe-inspiring. We stopped in Trinidad, and nothing seemed to go right. There was a sign on the road across from the Visitor Center, directing RVs to a parking lot a block away, but an illegally parked eighteen-wheeler hid it, so I pulled into the Visitor Center parking lot, which was a mistake. The entrance curves around behind the building, and isn't suited for an RV the size of ours. I shouldn't have attempted it, but we could have managed if there wasn't a Chevy Suburban with a travel trailer parked with its rear end sticking out into the driveway, blocking the way. I tried to maneuver around, backed up as much as I could, and scraped a tire and rim up on the curb, but we were stuck, with our right front bumper within inches of the trailer.

Miss Terry went into the Visitor Center to try and locate the owners of the Suburban, but they weren't there. Finally, after a lot of frustration and short tempers, we noticed movement inside the travel trailer. Miss Terry knocked on the door, and it turned out the owners had been sitting inside all along, having lunch! I guess they never noticed that huge RV up against their side, or the red-faced guy behind the wheel trying to get on with his life. Even in RV-land, some of our citizens have no consideration for their fellow man.

With the roadway finally cleared, we managed to find the RV parking lot, and parked next to a gaily painted bus conversion that

Meandering Down The Highway

I fell in love with. The whole exterior of the bus-turned-RV was painted like a patchwork quilt. We never saw the owners, but I'd have loved to see the inside of the rig.

The girl working the counter at Taco Bell in Trinidad was either having a bad day, or was maybe one taco short of a combination plate. When we ordered lunch, I asked her if the little dog Taco Bell uses in its television commercials was working, because I wanted an autograph.

"What dog?"

"You know, the cute little Chihuahua! From television!"

"Huh?"

"Yeah, the dog in all the TV commercials. Is he here? I've always wanted to meet him."

"Huh? What dog?"

Either they don't have television in Trinidad, Colorado, or my brand of humor doesn't work there, I'm not sure which. We took our food back to to the RV and ate lunch.

Later, someone told me that Trinidad is the sex change capitol of the world, and I remember reading a magazine article somewhere about a doctor there that performs a huge number of cross-gender procedures. Gee, and all we wanted was lunch and a handful of tourism brochures.

We ran into more of the unavoidable road construction through Colorado and were held up by two traffic accidents blocking the highway. There are a ton of places in Colorado I want to get back to, including the Air Force Academy in Colorado Springs, but we wanted to get to Torrington, Wyoming for a visit with Miss Terry's daughter, son and grandkids before we had to be in Idaho, so we kept on going. I had heard terrible things about congested traffic in Denver, but we arrived about 7:30 and it was no problem at all. Still a lot of vehicles on the road at that time of the evening, but traffic flowed smoothly.

We ran into more road construction north of Fort Collins,

Meandering Down The Highway

including a long stretch of two-way traffic along a narrow, rough section that continued into Wyoming. We promised ourselves again to avoid night driving as much as we could in the future.

Gassing up at the Flying J in Cheyenne, we were pleased to see that our gas mileage had improved to nearly 8 miles per gallon. It was cool enough that we hadn't had to use the air conditioning all day, and Interstate 25 is much smoother that I-40, which may had helped improve our economy. Still not good for a vehicle, but for a house it's not bad mileage, right?

Flying J had a big sign touting their 24 ounce T-bone steak, and I began drooling, so we decided it was time for dinner. If the steer that steak came from was a tough as the meat was, I *really* don't want to mess with the fellow who butchered it!

It was only another hour or so into Torrington, but we had had enough of traffic and night driving, so we pulled the RV into a dirt lot behind the truck stop and called it a day. It was a good thing too, because the next morning when we set off, we found the road construction even worse. A detour took us off I-25 and through Cheyenne, down narrow residential streets where the construction signs and light posts reached out, trying to scrape the sides off the RV. After five miles or so of tight negotiating on city streets, we were back on the interstate, a mile north of where we left it! Heading north, the exit we needed was blocked, and signs directed us to the next exit, which was also blocked! I finally made an illegal crossover, headed back south, and managed to find an exit that put us on Highway 85 going toward our destination.

This part of eastern Wyoming is mostly rolling hill country, with lots of farming and ranching operations. Miss Terry's sharp eyes spotted several hawks and antelope, which she pointed out to me. We passed cattle, farm trucks, and off in the distance tractors were working.

One of the best bargains we've seen on the road is the Goshen

Meandering Down The Highway

County Fairgrounds in Torrington. We arrived Friday morning, and for only $8 a day we got full hookups, and had the place pretty much to ourselves. There are about twenty RV spaces, but we were the only ones there. Mary Lu Pollat runs the fairgrounds office and is a real nice lady, laid back and easy to get along with. She lives in a house right on the premises and is always handy whenever a road weary RVer shows up.

We had arrived in town in time to attend a birthday party for Miss Terry's grandson, Tanner. Son Shawn and his wife, also named Shawn, have five active little boys, and they kept their grandma busy giving hugs, sharing ice cream and cake, looking at all of their little treasures, and hearing about their adventures in Little League and T-Ball.

This whole Shawn/Shawn thing confuses the heck out of me. Miss Terry named her oldest son Shawn, and then he went and married a girl named Shawn. I never know who is who when the family mentions them. I have to preface everything with "boy-Shawn" and "girl-Shawn" for clarification. Can you imagine the trouble I could get into - "Shawn sure looks pretty today, what a beauty" - or "I see Shawn must be working out, look at those muscles." It just puts too much strain on my limited mental capacities. From now on I'm calling them Thelma and Louise.

Miss Terry's granddaughter Libby was suffering from a bad cold, and the little one took a while to warm up to us, but once she did, she sure was a chatterbox. At just two, you can already see that Libby is going to be a knockout, just like her mom, Kelly, and grandma. I sure married into a family of fine looking women.

They were setting up a circus at the fairgrounds Saturday morning, so I wandered over and tried not to get in the way. The Culpepper & Merriweather Circus is based in Queen Creek, Arizona and is on the road performing eight months of the year, from March to October. Elephant handler Bryan Schoening told me they do two shows a day, seven days a week, and after five

Meandering Down The Highway

years he still loves it.

"I never take a day off, I'm here with the elephants seven days a week," Bryan said. The circus has two African elephants, Barbara and Connie. Fourteen year old Barbara is a bit of a ham when she sees a camera, and was happy to pose for a photograph.

"So how does a guy become an elephant handler?" I asked Bryan. "I ran away to join the circus," he replied. "and they didn't have anyone to operate the shovel, so I got that job. I've sort of dug my way up from there." Bryan said the elephants are remarkable animals, who respond very well to love and positive reinforcement. "It's all about nice words and treats," he told me. When it comes to treats, these pachyderms have insatiable appetites. Bryan said they go through 150 pounds of feed a day, and 75 gallons of water. I got out of there before they put *me* to work on the shovel!

I ran into Nicollette Johnson in the office trailer, and *I* was ready to run away and join the circus. A good looking, tall, leggy blonde, Nicollette said traveling with the circus is a great life.

"You're never bored," Nicollette explained. "Circus time is different from real time. We do a day show and an evening show, and have six hours or so off in between." Nicollette has been with the circus four years, traveling in a fifth wheel trailer with her eighteen year old daughter, who works with Bryan with the animals. Her sixteen year old son was off school for the summer and traveling with them as well. By the time the season is over, the circus will have played in every state west of Missouri. Not a bad way to spend your life, getting paid to travel in an RV.

Sunday, July 4th, the Torrington Volunteer Fire Department put on a fireworks display from the National Guard Armory right next door to the fairgrounds, giving us a great view of the show. The fireworks only lasted about ten minutes, donations being rather skimpy this year, but it was a good show while it lasted.

The Oregon Trail runs through this part of Wyoming, and

Meandering Down The Highway

there are several historical markers in the area giving information about the emigrants who traveled overland in their homes on wheels, seeking a better life. I kind of related to those early folks, in their forerunners to our modern day RVs, though I'm very appreciative of the things we have today to make our journeys easier and more comfortable - things like air conditioning, microwave ovens, and hot showers.

Adventures In Cowboy Country

One day we drove up to Fort Laramie, a National Historic Site administered by the National Park Service. The fort played an integral part in the expansion of the west, and many of the old buildings have been restored. There are great displays of life on the frontier, and several volunteers and seasonal workers in period costume are on hand to tell you what it was like to serve and live on a western military outpost in that historic period.

Bill Frazey was working in the trading post. It's obvious that Bill, a seasonal worker for the Park Service, loves his job. Within moments he took us on a mind trip back through time to the days when Fort Laramie was a living Army post.

"Just lean back there on the counter and look over there across the room," Bill told us. "They're all there - Kit Carson, Jim Bridger, Red Cloud, Sheridan, General Custer. During their time, they all traded right here in this room. Do you hear the bugler calling the troops to formation? Can you smell the horses and hear the jingle of equipment?" I swear, I could feel their presence as Bill talked.

Fort Laramie is also supposed to be haunted, and if one is inclined to believe that spirits walk among us, I can't think of a better place than one with all that history attached to it. There have been reports of the ghost of a calvary trooper who wanders the upper floors of the restored barracks, sitting on the bunks or poking among the equipment on display. Visitors and Park Service workers claim to have caught glimpses of the specter or

Meandering Down The Highway

heard his lonesome harmonica playing around the old barracks. Maybe he's just waiting for his comrades from so long ago to return from a patrol?

I don't have any fear of ghosts, but snakes can really get my skin crawling. Back in the old days, before Miss Terry got me civilized and housebroken, I pretty much shot every snake I came into contact with. I know, I know, they're part of the bigger scheme of things and it's not right to kill something just because we don't understand it, but you just let me have my little phobias and I'll leave you to yours, okay?

With the visitor packet they hand you at Fort Laramie is a flyer warning you that snakes are frequently found in the area. Sure enough, while we were poking around the fort, I stepped into one of the cells of the old guardhouse and encountered about the biggest snake I've seen in years. He was at least as thick as my arm, and Miss Terry said he probably went six or seven feet minimum. I couldn't tell you that for sure, I was too busy clawing my way past her to safety. Forget all that nonsense you've heard about women and children first - us survivors know it's every man for himself when the chips are down. Did you ever see a fat bald guy doing the backward broad jump while screaming at the top of his lungs? It's not a pretty sight.

On Wednesday, July 7, the urge to get back on the road was just too strong, so we got ready to hit the highway. It was bound to happen sooner or later, but that doesn't make it any easier - after driving the motorhome over 2,000 miles through city traffic, freeways, winding mountain passes, and rough construction zones, I managed to ding up the RV in the middle of the fairgrounds, and the only excuse I can claim is negligence, because we were all alone in a huge parking area and I have no one else to blame for my inattention. Pulling out of our parking slot at the fairgrounds, I turned the wheel too soon and swung the back end of the RV into one of the concrete barrier posts, breaking off

Meandering Down The Highway

a chunk of molding. The damage was fairly minor, but I felt terrible. I have to give Miss Terry credit, I know she wanted to cry, or beat me over the head with the handiest rock, but she just smiled (feebly) and said "accidents happen" as she surveyed the damage. If I had allowed myself just another four inches or so before I started my turn, we would have been okay. You can bet I'll be more careful in the future. As we've met more and more fulltimers, we've learned that until you ding your rig up at least once, you're not really considered a pro.

Guernsey, Wyoming, on Highway 26 about twenty miles west of Torrington, doesn't seem to have much going on, except for being the home of a huge Wyoming National Guard base. I would imagine that when the Guardsmen are at the base for training, they outnumber the locals about ten to one. But Guernsey is the site of two great historical sites - the Oregon Trail Ruts and Register Cliff.

A Park Ranger at Fort Laramie had advised me to leave our RV in Guernsey and drive our dinghy to the sites, but as it turned out all the advice did was make more work for us. The roads and parking lots at both places would have accommodated our rig easily.

We followed signs from the highway, crossed the North Platte river, and unhooked the Toyota in a pull-off, leaving the RV. Less than a half mile from the bridge, on a wide, well graded gravel road, is the parking area for the Oregon Trail Ruts. Here the wheels of thousands and thousands of wagons wore deep ruts, some as much as five feet deep into the soft sandstone, that still remain today. To see and stand in those ruts really gives you a connection to those pioneers and the hardships they endured.

There are several signs and information displays at the site, telling about the history of the area. Not only was this part of Wyoming important for its connection to the Oregon Trail and the Indian Wars, it was also part of the route of the Pony Express, the 49ers Gold Trail, and the old Mormon Trail. So much of what we

Meandering Down The Highway

read about as kids and saw fictionalized in movies and on television happened right where we were standing! It was really something to feel and experience.

Less than two miles from the bridge, on another good graded road, is Register Cliff, where thousands of emigrants, 49ers, soldiers, mountain men and others paused to carve their names. Unfortunately, over the years thousands of later visitors have done the same, and many of the earlier inscriptions have been damaged or obliterated. But you can still see many of the names and dates, stretching back as far as the mid-1800s. There is a small cemetery at the site, holding the unmarked graves of several pioneers who died along the rough route west.

Just as you cross the bridge over the river, there is a very pretty city park and golf course, with several campsites right along the river. We saw five or six RVs parked there, and if we hadn't wanted to get a few more miles behind us, it would have been a good place to spend a couple of days.

Back on Interstate 25, we traveled north through some very pretty country. Johnson County, Wyoming, where sheep ranchers and cattlemen went to battle during the Johnson County War, seemed pretty quiet except for a few thunderstorms off in the distance.

We pulled into Sheridan, Wyoming, and I found another neat town I could spend a lot of time in. Historic old downtown Sheridan looks like a scene from a 1950s movie, with a real hometown feel to it. We were headed to the local Wal-Mart to boondock in their parking lot when I spotted several RVs parked in a nice little city park. Washington Park has about six or seven RV spots among big trees, with picnic tables, restrooms and a dump station. A river flows alongside the park, and after we parked and got situated, Miss Terry and I crossed a little footbridge and strolled down a paved pathway along the river.

There was some traffic noise, but it pretty much quieted

Meandering Down The Highway

down about 11 p.m. and we slept until about 2 a.m., when a strong gust of wind slammed the motorhome, waking me up and sending thoughts of uprooted trees crashing down on the RV through my brain. The windstorm was brief, but intense, and after a half hour or so things calmed down and I fell back asleep.

The next morning we crossed the border into Montana, and about 60 miles north of Sheridan entered the country where George Armstrong Custer and the Seventh Cavalry had their fateful encounter with the Plains Indians in 1873. We first stopped at Garyowen, a small museum and gift shop about three miles south of Little Bighorn Battlefield National Monument. The museum has a display of artifacts about the Indian Wars and a video that gives a lot of information on the Battle of the Little Bighorn, also known as Custer's Last Stand.

Driving into the National Monument, we found the place packed and parking impossible. We backtracked and left the RV at the Little Bighorn Casino, driving the mile or so back to the monument in the pickup. The day before, while gassing up in Buffalo, Wyoming, some folks had spotted our *Gypsy Journal* signs on the camper and Terry gave them a copy. Who should we happen to run into at the monument but the same couple! What's that they say about small worlds?

Besides being the site of Custer's Last Stand, the monument includes the Custer National Cemetery, where close to 5,000 of our servicemen from all wars, along with their wives, civilians, and Indian Scouts are buried. It was a moving experience to walk on such hallowed ground and read the names on some of the headstones. So many have given so much so that the rest of us can have the freedom we enjoy today.

The park rangers gave two great talks, one on the life of the Plains Indians and another on the history and events that led up to the infamous Battle of the Little Bighorn. It was interesting to hear some facts that we never learned in grade school, and to

Meandering Down The Highway

realize that there really were no good guys or bad guys, there were just two sides, each doing what they believed they had to do. The Indians were fighting to preserve their land and culture and their way of life, while the soldiers were just as committed to furthering westward expansion. Both sides were willing to die for what they believed in, and men on both sides did. After touring the museum, we walked up Last Stand Hill to the mass grave where 220 men who died with Custer are buried, then down along the footpath through the battlefield. Small tombstones mark the spots where troopers died. It's a sobering experience. I felt a special kinship with those men who struggled there so long ago - a little less than a hundred years later I also served in the Seventh Cavalry, though instead of horses, we rode helicopters into the field. Like those old troopers from another time, I still feel a ripple of pride when I hear our old marching song, *Gary Owen.*

    During our visit to the Little Bighorn, the wind really began to blow, so much so that while one of the Park Rangers was giving a presentation on the Indian way of life, the wind pulled the tent stakes out of the ground and the tent the crowd was sitting under began to collapse. Myself and several other men found ourselves hanging onto the guy ropes to keep the thing upright long enough that people could get out. No one was injured, but a few people in the crowd got a thrill or two and a good story to take back home to the folks in Des Moines.

    Back on the interstate, the wind continued getting worse and it was a constant battle to keep the motorhome in one lane. Every time a massive gust would hit us, that big wall of fiberglass acted like a sail and the RV wanted to leave the roadway or slide into the lane next to us - the lane usually occupied by a fast moving semi. Some RVs were passing us, seemingly unaffected by the wind, but I'm still too new at driving this huge thing to have their confidence, I guess. I remembered what one of the skilled race car

Meandering Down The Highway

drivers at our little speedway back home told me the first time I climbed inside a stock car to compete - "Just drive your own race and let the other guy drive his." (He also told me the secret to winning a race was simple, "haul a## and turn left." The advice worked, I won the first race I entered.) I took his advice again, and drove the RV the way I was comfortable with given the road conditions. Overall, I've found that on the interstates I get the best mileage and the most comfortable ride between 55 and 60 miles per hour. Even though a lot of traffic flies past me, that's where I seem to have the best trip. Besides, this isn't about racing, it's about seeing the country at a pace slow enough to enjoy it.

We finally made Billings, refueled and pulled into the Cracker Barrel General Store for an early dinner. The food was great, and the manager said we were welcome to stay in the back of their parking lot overnight. Gratefully, we accepted the offer and called it a day. We hadn't covered many miles this day, but we saw some interesting things and we were even happier to have our home on wheels when we needed a refuge from the wind.

Friday morning dawned clear and calm, the wind having blown itself out overnight. We pointed the nose of our RV west on Interstate 90 and began a long day of driving, hoping to make it to Kamiah, Idaho and the Lewis-Clark Resort by nightfall. Terry's folks are members of Lewis-Clark and have had good things to say about the resort and the surrounding countryside.

Gasoline in Montana was the most expensive so far on our trip - as much as $1.36 a gallon in Missoula. (Later, in Oregon and Washington, we would fondly remember those low gasoline prices.) We drove from Billings to Butte, stopped in the Flying J for lunch, and it seemed like we were holding a Pace Arrow Vision owners rally. While we were eating, a unit identical to ours pulled up to the gas pumps. Within moments two matching 1997 models also parked on the lot. We all stood around comparing notes and experiences for a few minutes. The fellow in the twin

Meandering Down The Highway

rig to ours had just discovered that the upper right corner of his passenger windshield had pulled away from the frame, leaving a gap several inches long. With the proper tools, Miss Terry could have reset it, but after looking at the damage, she and the owner agreed it would be wiser to get it into a full service glass shop, so he headed off in search of help.

Just east of Missoula, Miss Terry spotted a sign for the Rock Creek Lodge reading *"Testicle Festival, Come And Have A Ball"* She said it had to do with something called Rocky Mountain oysters, which result from doing really rude things to cattle. Taking no chances, I crossed my legs and kept on driving.

Scenic Byways And Wild Rivers

Missoula, Montana was a town of high gasoline prices, heavy traffic, and rude people. We found ourselves needing to change lanes after somehow straying off Highway 12, and the drivers of the cars flying past us made it plain they considered making way for a lost out-of-towner an act akin to national treason. I think they were trying to point me toward Highway 1, since so many held up just one finger as they passed.

The Wal-Mart in Missoula looked like an RV park when we passed at about 5:30 p.m., with several rigs boondocking. When we gassed up, the only friendly person in Missoula told us it was about a hundred miles to our destination. He was friendly, just not all that accurate. By the time we shut off the motor in Kamiah, our odometer said we had traveled over 150 miles

But oh, what a 150 miles it was! I've been in every state except Utah, and a handful of foreign countries, but I don't think I've ever seen a stretch of landscape as pretty as the route along Highway 12 over Lolo Pass and down into Idaho. Towering mountains, a wild river running alongside the highway for the entire length of the trip, and sights that make your heart smile around every bend in the road. Everywhere you look, it's like a scene from a calendar.

Meandering Down The Highway

Highway 12 through this area is a National Scenic Byway, and every RVer or serious road warrior should make this drive at least once. It's full of twists and turns, and the faint of heart might feel a flutter or two, but just gear down, keep your speed down, sit back and enjoy the ride. The highway follows the old Lewis and Clark Trail and the country looks very much like what those early day explorers must have experienced on their journey through the area 200 years ago. For a portion of the way, the road also follows the route the Nez Perce Indians used in their flight from the United States Army as they tried to take refuge in Canada. After a valiant effort, and undergoing severe hardships, the Indians finally were forced to surrender in Montana, just miles from the safety of the border.

Just as we crossed into Idaho, a beautiful mule deer doe greeted us from alongside the highway. There was still a lot of daylight left, and just too much spectacular scenery to be in a hurry, so we took our time, pulled over here and there to let traffic pass or to take a picture, and pulled into Kamiah about 8:30 p.m. after 13 hours on the road, covering over 500 miles.

Lewis-Clark Resort sits in a gorgeous spot in the Kamiah Valley, with the Clearwater River flowing by just across the highway. When explorers Lewis and Clark came through the area they pronounced the valley paradise, and it truly is. The resort features everything from a swimming pool and spa to a fishing pond, laundry, small convenience store, and restaurant. They even have a motel, in case you have friends or family who want to meet you for a visit. The place was packed, and we arrived without reservations, but they found a spot for us and we settled in for for a couple of nights rest before heading the 100 miles or so up to Moscow for the Life on Wheels Conference. After several nights boondocking, it was nice to have a dump station and hookups. When we expanded our two slideouts, we were amazed how much room we had after the somewhat cramped

Meandering Down The Highway

quarters of the last couple of nights.

Saturday morning we wandered around the park for a bit, then drove to the Farmers Market in nearby Kooskia, where Miss Terry got a great deal on some fresh homemade bread and produce. From there we stopped in Kamiah to visit her Uncle Roy Dotson and Aunt Diane at their home. Then it was a quick stop at the local grocery to stock up, and back to the RV. While Terry caught up on laundry, I fired up the computer and knocked out some work, knowing that the next week was going to be very busy and I probably wouldn't find much time to write.

The Kamiah Valley is a delight, and I really liked the town of Kamiah. The town's short main street can best be described as Western/Victorian, with false fronted buildings that I really liked.

From Kamiah to Lewiston, Idaho is about 60 miles, and every bit of it gorgeous as we rolled along Sunday morning. There are lots of pullouts to stop and see the Clearwater River as it flows past or to let faster traffic get by so you can take your time and enjoy the view. Idaho has a lot of history to it, and historic markers dot every road we traveled on. I have a hard time passing these wayside information signs without stopping, but finally Miss Terry convinced me that if I didn't keep on driving we'd never get anywhere. Turning north on Highway 95 at Lewiston, it's about 38 miles into Moscow. The climb up Lewiston Hill is steep and slow, but the view is fantastic. Looking down on the city and surrounding farmlands below, you'd swear you were in an airplane.

Moscow, Idaho was a delight, set in rolling hill country with farm fields all around, and the University of Idaho campus is beautiful. In the six days we were in Moscow, every local we met was friendly and went out of their way to make all of us RVers feel welcome.

Back To School

A report on the Life on Wheels Conference is included in this

Meandering Down The Highway

issue, so I won't go into a lot of details about the course itself, except to say that anyone who owns an RV or is even thinking of purchasing one should consider the week spent attending the conference a must. I've devoted hundreds of hours to reading about RVing, researching on the Internet, and talking to other RVers, and I was still overwhelmed at the shear magnitude of information available. There are over 100 classes in everything from boondocking to trailer towing to getting the most use out of your equipment. Was it worth our time? Before many of our classmates were back at their RVs after the closing ceremony on Friday afternoon, Miss Terry and I had made our reservations to attend next year!

There were nearly 600 RVers attending Life on Wheels, in everything from plush $300,000 luxury rigs to pop-up campers, but there wasn't a snob in the bunch. When we arrived Sunday afternoon there was an open house, and many of the students had opened their RVs for others to look at and ask questions. Terry and I stopped in to admire a gorgeous Winnebago and met Bob and Lynn Throckmorton from Hemet, California, two of the nicest people we've ever run into. Lynn's a real sweetheart, but it's obvious Bob's the smarter of the two, since he sure married a better class of person than she did. They made us feel welcome, and in no time at all it felt like we'd been frends forever. In fact, the last day of the conference, Bob told us if we were ever in their part of the world, to be sure and stop in. Now, I know that's just something folks say to be polite, but old Bob's sure going to be surprised one morning when he stumbles outside for his morning newspaper and finds us camped out on his lawn.

One real treat for me was to meet our instructors, many of whom are the top experts in the field of RVing and are well known for their books and articles on the subject. Gaylord Maxwell, founder of Life on Wheels, has been a columnist for *Motorhome* magazine for eighteen years and is *the* authority when it comes to

Meandering Down The Highway

this wonderful lifestyle we've chosen. Also on hand to share their knowledge were such well known writers and experts as Bill Farlow, Joe and Vicki Kieva, Mike and Pam Steffen, and my own heroine, Sharlene "Charlie" Minshall. The classes were great, and there was something going on every evening to keep us busy. One night a great singer/cowboy poet entertained us, another we were treated to a delicious salmon bake while local high school musicians performed, and on yet another night we attended a splendid musical called *Beehive* performed by the Idaho Repertory Theatre. The performance was fabulous, full of energy and action, and by the time it was over everyone in the crowd was out of their seats clapping and stomping their feet. Each night we fell into bed exhausted, our heads swimming with all the new knowledge and experiences, only to drag ourselves out the next morning, ready to learn even more.

There's not a flabby student at the University of Idaho. As I mentioned, the place is beautiful, but everything is either uphill or downhill (actually, it seemed like *everything* was uphill!) and our legs sure paid the price in aching muscles by the end of a long day. I had to lay in an extra stock of chocolate ice cream and potato chips just to maintain my weight after all that exercise!

We put a couple of stacks of newspapers in the information tent, and were really thrilled by the reception the *Gypsy Journal* received. During the week many of our fellow students stopped us to make favorable comments, and by the time the conference was over we had sold several subscriptions. I also got a chance to check my e-mail, and had messages from quite a few folks who had received complimentary copies, telling me that they wanted to subscribe.

One thing that impressed us at the Life on Wheels conference was the number of younger people attending classes. There were quite a few baby boomers, and several students even younger. The youngest was a boy about eight or nine years old, attending

Meandering Down The Highway

every class with his parents, ages 30 and 31. They are in the process of selling their home and getting ready to hit the road, home schooling their son as they travel. A good number of the students came to Life on Wheels before they even bought an RV, getting all the knowledge they could beforehand. We used to think of RVers, especially fulltimers, as retired folks, but there are many thousands of younger people out there enjoying life on the road. Henry and Linda Butler, fellow students and Escapees, are just one example of a couple living the good life.

Computers are becoming an important part of life on the road, and more and more RVers are using them for writing, communications, and to handle such chores as online banking and monitoring their investments. Several people were discussing having custom computer desks built to fit into their RVs, but when we showed them the off the shelf desk we use, there was a run on the local Staples office supply store. I was tempted to stop in and ask the manager for a commission.

Friday afternoon the conference wrapped up, but we stayed an extra night to do some interviews and avoid the rush getting out of town. Miss Terry loves Mexican food, and we discovered a really good restaurant called Mercado Family Restaurant and Cantina. The food and service were both excellent, and Miss Terry says it's now on her list of places we can't miss the next time we're in town, and you can bet we'll be back to Moscow again.

I've been hearing a lot about the new GPS (global satellite positioning) systems and all the benefits they hold for RVers. Saturday morning one of the students parked near us, Dave Baleria from Medford, Oregon, demonstrated his GPS for me, and it was impressive. I'm not sure I'm smart enough to operate one of these newfangled gadgets myself (I'm still confused by handheld calculators, and the thought of programming a VCR gives me a migraine), but I can see how useful one would be to

Meandering Down The Highway

most people. Dave and his wife Sandy are working their way toward becoming fulltimers, and we shared a thought or two about life on the open road. Dave also gave me a couple of tips on good campgrounds to check out when we get over to the Oregon coast.

We pulled out Saturday morning, stopped by the fairgrounds to dump our holding tanks (the fairgrounds also has a few RV hookups) and then went over to have our rig weighed by Neil and Pat LeKander from A'Weigh We Go, a company that conducts weight and safety classes for RVers at Life on Wheels and other RV events across the country. We were dreading the news, sure that our rig was grossly overweight with all the things we've crammed into every nook and cranny. When we found out that we were actually only about 500 pounds over our limit it was a relief, though we will have to do some trimming and eliminating. The bad news was that we learned about yet another lie the dealer who sold us our rig had told us. The salesman assured us we had a 5,000 pound capacity hitch, and it turns out that it's really only rated at 3500 pounds. Folks, do your homework and don't believe everything you're told by a salesman in search of a big commission. There are a lot of very honest, reputable RV dealers and sales representatives out there, but the grass also holds its share of snakes.

The drive up Lewiston Hill is steep. For a new RVer still unsure of himself, going back downhill was downright scary! Fortunately the road is a divided four lane highway and traffic was light. By gearing down and gentle use of the brakes now and then, we made it down in fine shape, except for that layer or two of tooth enamel I ground off.

We returned to Lewis-Clark Resort in Kamiah to join, since no one from the business office was available when we visited over the previous weekend. Membership is a good bargain, we get 28 days a year free camping at the resort, and it makes us

Meandering Down The Highway

eligible to join Coast to Coast and RPI, two membership camping groups that can save fulltimers a fortune over the course of a year on the road.

Just as we entered Kamiah, I saw a helicopter with a fire bucket slung below, and at the same time spotted a massive cloud of smoke. The fire was at a lumberyard just outside of town, and had spread to a nearby hill, but the professionals seemed to have everything in control, so we kept on going, arriving at Lewis-Clark just in time to set up and get ready to attend a street dance in the resort. We were assigned to the same camping site we had the weekend before, and Don and Jan Dotson, neighbors who had the space next to us then, were still there and greeted us warmly. It's quickly becoming apparent that our fellow RVers are becoming a sort of extended family that we'll run into over and over as we travel.

Destination: Oregon Coast

We spent three days at Lewis-Clark Resort resting up from our busy week in Moscow and completing the details for resort membership and getting enrolled in Coast to Coast and RPI. On Tuesday we left, driving west on Highway 12 toward Washington state. The rolling Palouse wheat country seemed to go on forever, golden hills stretching out as far as the eye could see. Coming into Walla Walla, there were stands offering onions for sale all along the highway.

When I was a kid, one of my favorite books was the story of the Sager children, seven youngsters who were orphaned when their parents died of cholera while the family was traveling on the Oregon Trail. Through the help of a kind fellow traveler and their own tenacity, the pioneer children managed to survive and continue on their perilous journey, eventually arriving at the mission run by Marcus and Narcissa Whitman just outside present day Walla Walla. The missionary couple adopted the children, and I would like to say the story ended with everyone

Meandering Down The Highway

living happily ever after. But life is not a fairy tale - in reality, the local Indians turned against the missionaries several years later, massacring the Whitmans and the two Sager boys, along with several others at the mission. The Sager girls were taken captive and later ransomed. Today the Whitman Mission National Historic Site includes displays depicting life in the Whitmans' time, the troubles with the Indians and the tragic events at the mission. A path from the visitor center leads to a monument atop a nearby hill dedicated to the missionaries and the grave where the massacre victims are buried.

We arrived at Whitman Mission late in the day, just as the only other visitors were leaving. The friendly young woman working the counter answered several questions for us, then we set out to wander around the site. It was so peaceful strolling through the grounds that it was hard to accept the tragedies the place had been witness to.

If overnight parking had been allowed at the mission, we would have loved to camp right there for the evening, but we continued onward instead, turning onto Highway 730 to cross into Oregon. This was a special occasion for Miss Terry, since Oregon was the last of the lower 48 states for her to visit. Highway 730 is narrow and runs alongside the Columbia River, and the trucks seemed to be more than willing to run over an RV if it didn't get out of their way fast enough. We had a strange event happen - we were passing a weigh station and slowed down for a truck pulling back onto the highway. Moments later there was a flash and loud bang at the curb side of our RV and I was certain we'd suffered a blowout. Pulling over to the side of the road quickly, we couldn't find anything wrong with the tires, the propane tank or the rest of the RV. We finally concluded the only explanation could be that the trucker had thrown a firecracker out of his window as he passed us. We were really happy to pull into the Umatilla Marina and RV Park and leave the highway to the

Meandering Down The Highway

eighteen-wheelers for the night.

Umatilla was a very pleasant surprise. The town doesn't look like much coming in from the east, but the city-owned RV park sits right on the Columbia River, with large parking spaces, lots of trees and grass, and the place was very clean. Full hookups were only $15 a night. Though the RV park sits close to the Interstate 82 bridge over the Columbia River, it was surprisingly quiet and we had a restful night.

The next morning we stopped at the Oregon Welcome Center near the marina, where Helen Stanley and Kathi Wahlert loaded us up with brochures and information. If these two are any indication of the people from Oregon, it's really a friendly place. They definitely made us feel welcome. We crossed the river back into Washington state and drove west along Highway 14, stopping at the Stonehenge Memorial, a replica of the ancient stone structure in England. Constructed by Sam Hill, a Quaker businessman who was appalled by the tragic loss of life in World War I, the monument is dedicated to Klickitat County veterans who lost their lives in service to the country in the conflict. At the site is also a monument to those who fell in World War II, Korea and Vietnam.

It was sad to see all those names of young men who died before they ever had a chance to experience life. We came away asking ourselves "Why?"

The drive down the wide Columbia River is a trip everyone should make. Crossing the river back into Oregon just east of The Dalles, we parked in a small city park near the Chamber of Commerce, and arrived just minutes before the office closed. The girl on duty allowed us to browse for a few minutes, but made it plain we were going to be keeping her after hours. We hurriedly grabbed a handful of pamphlets and returned to the RV, where we had a quick snack of cheese and crackers. We would have liked to have lingered longer in The Dalles, but the park was quickly

Meandering Down The Highway

filling up for a softball game and we were taking up several parking spaces, so we left.

Our next stop was Multnomah Falls, a dramatic waterfall just east of Portland. We hiked up the trail to the bridge just below the falls and joined several other visitors enjoying nature's beauty. It was an ideal spot, but the day was fading fast and we had a long way to go yet. Even at 8 p.m. traffic in Portland was still pretty heavy, but we managed to get through the city and onto Highway 26 headed toward the coast.

After the rather treeless countryside of eastern Oregon, nearing the coast, with all its greenery was a real treat. Climbing into the Coast Range, we pulled into a pullout to make way for slower traffic and spotted an interesting RV, a shingle-sided house built onto the back of an early 1960s era Dodge three ton truck. Quite a rustic looking setup. We chatted with the owner a while. He wasn't eager to share his name, but did tell us he's been living in the rig fulltime for eight years.

Darkness closed in on us before we expected, and as we topped the mountain range, we had a real scare. I backed off the throttle to move into the right lane in a passing zone, and a big ball of flame shot out the side of our rig. We made a panic stop on the road shoulder and bailed out with fire extinguishers while a passing motorist stopped to offer to call 911. But nothing was on fire, and just as the day before, we couldn't find any explanation. I finally decided that the problem may have been backfiring through our exhaust pipe, which is located on the same side of the RV. We drove on to a nearby rest area and parked for a few minutes to calm our nerves.

Because of the delays with the RV, we didn't get into our destination, Seaside, Oregon, until late Wednesday night. Every RV park we saw was closed and we were exhausted. I stopped at the police station to inquire about a place to park overnight and the dispatcher was very adamant that we not park inside the city

Meandering Down The Highway

limits, at the risk of a citation. She directed us to a paved parking area at Del Ray Beach, just north of town on Highway 101.

Apparently the dispatcher hasn't been to Del Ray Beach in some time, because after we swung into the parking lot, we discovered that the pavement was buried under about two feet of beach sand. With no place to back out, we had no other choice but to make a U-turn and try to find another parking place. Well, we made it about halfway through our turn when the heavy RV ground to a halt, with sand over the bottom of the wheels. After the prerequisite whining and a few unfortunate words that would have surely made my Momma turn over in her grave, I retrieved the shovel from the RV's spare tire compartment and began to dig. Sometime around 2:30 a.m. we finally made it back onto the highway.

Knowing we were much too tired to drive on, I stopped at the first parking lot I spotted that would accommodate our RV, the Seaside Christian Center. Several young people were just pulling out of the parking lot, and when I explained our predicament, they said they were members of the church congregation and invited us to stay there as long as we needed to. Punch drunk, I took a quick shower and climbed into bed. Later during our visit, a sergeant with the Seaside Police Department told me their officers usually just direct RVers to a tire store parking lot on the south entrance to town. I wished we had run into him instead of talking to his dispatcher.

The next morning the church's youth minister arrived about 8 a.m. and I introduced myself and explained our presence. He welcomed us and said the church was pretty empty until Sunday morning and welcomed us to park for a couple of days if we wanted to. Though we appreciated the church's hospitality, we didn't want to abuse their kindness, and moved on to Circle Creek Campground, a couple of miles south of Seaside.

Circle Creek is a pretty family park, every space has it's own

Meandering Down The Highway

paved parking slot and picnic table, and trees and grass were abundant. We stayed four nights, and our only complaint about Circle Creek was the lack of water pressure. When the park filled up Friday afternoon we discovered simple chores like taking a shower or flushing the toilet became a long term activity.

I love beach towns, and Seaside and Cannon Beach have lots to offer. We walked along the water's edge, dancing out of the way of the surf, we browsed through little shops offering everything from souvenirs to salt water taffy, we watched kids building sand castles, and stuffed ourselves with seafood. A clerk in one of the stores in Seaside recommended we try Doogers Seafood, a couple of blocks from the beach. The food was so good we went back a second time during our stay in Seaside. Miss Terry and I agreed that if we ever decided to give up our life on the road, the Northwest coast is the place we'd choose to live.

Portland newscasts said that gasoline prices in Oregon are the highest in the nation - on the coast we paid $1.53 a gallon, and saw some stations where premium unleaded was going for $1.76. While we were there, the state legislature voted to add a five cent per gallon tax. Oregonians were talking about demanding the issue be put to a vote of the people, and it was obvious the price increase wasn't going to pass if the citizens had anything to say about it.

One day we drove the twenty miles or so into Astoria. We toured Fort Clatsop, where the Lewis and Clark expedition wintered after reaching the Pacific Ocean. We also drove through the city, admiring the wonderful old Victorian homes, and made the drive up the hill to the Astoria Column, which dominates the skyline and affords a 360 degree view of the entire area. As we neared the tower, Terry spotted a blacktail deer munching grass on the side of the hill. I grabbed a camera and began shooting film. The deer was apparently used to people, she allowed me to get within twenty or thirty feet of her as she grazed. It was thrilling to

Meandering Down The Highway

be so close to such a beautiful animal. After we toured the Column and started back downhill, sharp-eyed Terry sighted two more does and a spotted fawn, and again the deer allowed us to get close enough to snap photos.

Cheese, Classic Aircraft, Crabs And Clams

After a few days in Seaside, we wandered down the Pacific Coast Highway (Highway 101), passing through Tillamook, Lincoln City, and Depoe Bay before stopping for a few days at Newport. The vistas along the coast are wonderful, and we stopped frequently at scenic overlooks to drink in all of the wonderful sights.

In Tillamook, we toured the Tillamook Cheese Factory, sampled the fine cheeses they make there, and Miss Terry did some shopping at the factory store, stocking our larder with all sorts of tasty goodies. A few miles further down the highway, we stopped at the Tillamook Air Museum, which houses a fine collection of military and civilian aircraft, as well as flying paraphernalia from World War II. No veteran or aircraft enthusiast should pass this up. The museum also offers rides in vintage aircraft, for the really adventurous. The gift shop is a little spendy, but the museum is well worth the admission price.

In Lincoln City we were amazed at all of the kites people were flying, including one huge tunnel-shaped contraption that was so big it required a smaller parachute-shaped kite to keep it aloft. I found the best restaurant in the world in Lincoln City - Pier 101. We were attracted by two signs on the side of the restaurant, one reporting they didn't serve yuppie food and another stating that unruly children and poodles weren't allowed. The signs alone were reason enough to stop, but when we walked in and they were playing Jimmy Buffett on the stereo, I was hooked. (For those of you who don't already know it, Buffett is the greatest singer/songwriter in the world. Just ask me and I'll tell you.) As the hostess was seating us, she noticed the booth was a

Meandering Down The Highway

little tight for me and moved the table slightly. My evil sense of humor kicked in and I demanded to know if she thought I was fat. The poor girl turned about three shades of red, denied everything, and before I knew it she had served me a huge crab cocktail, on the house. A place where they play Jimmy Buffett, don't allow yuppies or poodles, and give me free food! It was nirvana. If you're on the coast, be sure you stop for a meal at Pier 101, and bring your appetite. The food was delicious and the portions were very ample.

Passing through Depoe Bay, we pulled off to take in the view and that eagle-eyed lady of mine spotted a whale! Grey whales migrate along the coast from Alaska to Baja, Mexico and are usually seen in the Spring and Fall, but a few hang out along the Oregon coast most of the year. There were several whale watching boats in the bay, and we spent a wonderful hour or so watching the whale frolic in the water. What an experience!

At the Visitors Center in Umatilla we had picked up a brochure offering two free nights at Leisure Time Resorts Whalers Rest Resort in Newport. The resort is located just across the highway from the ocean, and has tons of amenities, including a heated indoor pool, spa, two clubhouses, and a very friendly staff. There was a presentation on Leisure Time Resorts' eleven properties in the Pacific Northwest, and if we weren't planning to visit so many other parts of the country we very well may have bought a membership. As it is, we're just not sure we'll be spending enough time in any one region to make it pay off.

After our two days at Whalers Rest, we moved to the other side of Newport for a couple of days at Pacific Shores RV Resort. Even more luxurious than Whalers Rest, Pacific Shores backs up to the ocean, with two pools and spas, golf course, club house, and a magnificent view of the ocean and Yaquina Head lighthouse.

Newport has much to offer visitors, and we took in as much as we could while we were there, including the Oregon Coast

Meandering Down The Highway

Aquarium, Undersea Gardens, and long walks along the fishing docks and beach. Rockhounds hunt the beaches around Newport for agates, which can be found in abundance as the tide goes out. We picked up several in a stroll along the beach one afternoon. Newport is also considered the Dungeness crab capitol of the world, and locals and visitors alike love catching their own dinner. At low tides, seafood lovers can also dig their own clams. For those not into harvesting their own food from the sea, there are plenty of shops selling fresh seafood, or you can sometimes purchase directly from the fishing boats at the docks.

The weather along the coast was cool, with morning fog that burned away by midday, then closed in again in the early evening. Walking along the foggy beaches was almost surreal. It's a place we'll be returning to many times in the future.

We weren't in any hurry to leave Newport, but we had reservations for the Salem (Oregon) gun show the weekend of July 31 -August 1. Highway 20, going east from Newport, is a corkscrew for the first 25 or 30 miles as it climbs through the hills, but there were plenty of turnouts where we could pull over and allow traffic to get past us, so we just took our time and enjoyed the ride.

We got quite a scare in Corvallis - we were going through an intersection on the green light when a fellow on a bicycle rode directly into our path. I slammed on the brakes, hoping I could get our huge rig stopped in time to avoid running over him, His guardian angel must have been riding on the handle bars, because we managed to stop. I still don't know what he must have been thinking, he was stopped on the curb and looked directly at us, before pedaling into the roadway. I might be able to chalk it up to youthful ignorance if it was a kid, but this guy was in his mid-20s and should have been old enough to know better. I'm amazed at how many times cars have pulled out in front of us with no margin for error or safety. People just don't understand that these big

Meandering Down The Highway

vehicles don't stop on a dime.

The gun show in Salem was pretty much a bust, as far as sales go. We took in a few bucks, but not nearly as much as we'd hoped to. The State Fairgrounds, where the show was held, has a small parking area with RV electrical hookups, but no water or sewer. The lady working in the office told us a circus had stayed there earlier in the year and blown out all of their electrical hookups, but for $10 a night we could dry camp in a nice grove of oak trees adjacent to the RV area. Since it was convenient to the gun show, we paid for two nights. Looking back, I think we'd have been better off to find an RV park somewhere and pay a few more dollars.

Four or five RVs parked in the oak grove, so it was secure enough. But there were several piles of empty beer bottles and other trash lying around, evidence that maybe some street people use the area occasionally. Saturday night the place filled up with people going to a dance at the fairgrounds, which didn't start until about 10 p.m. and lasted into the wee hours of the morning. The noisy crowds coming and going, racing their engines and shining their headlights into the RVs made it hard to sleep for most of us.

Sunday afternoon, when the show ended, we discovered that some bright-thinking individual had locked all of the gates exiting the area where the RVs were parked. Finally a police officer cut a lock onto a side street so we could leave, but an illegally parked car made it impossible for us to pull out. I ended up jack-knifing the dinghy, then holding up traffic while we unhooked and got out of the street. Needless to say, the folks who manage the RV parking for the fairgrounds are not on my list of all-time favorite people.

We needed to stock up on a few supplies and hoped to get to Campers World in Wilsonville, Oregon, just south of Portland, before they closed Sunday. Between the time lost in trying to get a gate opened at the fairgrounds, then being jammed up pulling

Meandering Down The Highway

out, we made it to the store with about fifteen minutes to spare. I made a mad dash in one direction, while Terry went off in another, and we managed to get most of what we needed before they closed.

Wandering Through Washington

Crossing into Washington state on Interstate 5, we pulled into a rest stop a few miles north of the state line to empty our holding tanks. We really appreciate the fact that both Oregon and Washington are so RV friendly. Many rest stops and quite a few of the small towns we've visited have free dump stations. The sky was fairly clear, and we got a good view of Mount St. Helens, the volcano that blew her top and did so much destruction to the countryside almost 20 years ago.

We planned to stop in Longview, Washington to visit an old friend of mine but when we arrived we discovered that Don and his family were in Montana, where they had been involved in a head-on collision with a dump truck while on vacation. We were happy to learn that though they were banged up a bit, none of their injuries were life threatening. I talked to Don on the telephone and promised we'd catch up with him in a few weeks, when they were back home and feeling better,

Leaving Longview, we drove west on Highway 4 along the Columbia River. In the tiny town of Skamokawa we happened upon Skamokawa Vista Park, a facility operated by the Port of Skamokawa. This has to be one of the best kept secrets in Washington state. For $15 we got a site with a picnic table, cable TV, and electrical hookups, with water and a dump station just across the driveway. The park sits right on the bank of the Columbia River and has a small beach. As we were pulling in, a huge freighter was heading out to sea just a few yards offshore. Chuck Parker, a retired Air Force NCO, came by the next morning to collect our camping fee and chat a bit. Chuck told us that the name Skamokawa is an Indian word meaning "smoke on

Meandering Down The Highway

the water," a reference to the heavy fog that blankets the river at times.

We had reservations at Eagles Nest RV Resort, a Coast to Coast affiliate in Ilwaco, Washington. Eagles Nest sits on a hill, with a great view of the ocean and the Ilwaco boat harbor. The resort has all of the amenities one could ask for, and the staff is very friendly.

Ilwaco, on the Long Beach Peninsula, makes a good base for exploring the area. The 28 mile long peninsula affords excellent beaches, has a handful of small towns, and is a fun place to spend a few days or an entire summer. Several charter boats operate out of Ilwaco, there are two neat lighthouses, and Fort Canby State Park, as well as museums and miles of beach to explore. We went to the top of North Head Lighthouse, built in 1898 and still in operation. Bill and Carolyn Wahl are fulltime RVers who were volunteering at the lighthouse for the summer. Carolyn mans the desk downstairs, while Bill is up on top telling visitors about the history of the lighthouse and this part of the Washington coast.

One day we drove our pickup north to Raymond, Washington, where we stopped to admire the statue erected in honor of hometown hero Robert Bush, who won the Congressional Medal of Honor during World War II. I met Bob Bush years ago when I lived in Washington, and it was an honor to be around such a genuine hero.

When I was a much younger man, I lived in Aberdeen, Washington and operated newspapers in Grays Harbor. It had been almost twenty years since I had been back, so I was eager to visit the area and see what had changed and what was still the same.

Many of the fine old buildings in Aberdeen have been torn down due to neglect, but I was delighted to find the historic old building where I had my office and print shop still standing and completely refurbished. The old place has quite a history, at one

Meandering Down The Highway

time being the headquarters for Billy Ghoul, a notorious saloon keeper and outlaw who made it a practice to drug sailors who hit port with pockets full of pay, then drag them down a secret tunnel to the harbor's edge, where they were thrown into the water to drown. Downstairs was the saloon, while upstairs the building housed several cribs for prostitutes. Back in its wild past, Grays Harbor was known as the Port of Floating Men due to all of the unfortunate sailors Billy Ghoul and his henchmen murdered. There's an old saying, "if these old walls could talk, the stories they'd tell." I spent many a late night hour in that old building, and sometimes I almost believed those walls were telling me about all the tragedy they'd seen.

It was great to visit with some of my old friends in Aberdeen and her sister city of Hoquiam. We only got to spend a few hours there that first day, but since we planned to be in the area for a while, we promised to get together with them again soon.

We took the long way back to Ilwaco, driving out to the fishing town of Westport, then down Highway 105 through Grayland and North Cove and along the north side of Willapa Bay, home to several commercial oyster operations. South of Raymond a few miles we came across a huge herd of elk grazing in a meadow alongside the road. There must have been at least forty animals in the herd, and we pulled off to admire them in the fading light. Movies and stage productions are fine, but for real entertainment just show me a few wild critters in their natural habitat and leave me alone to enjoy watching them.

Okay, here's a tip for you if you love good pizza. Go to Bubba's Pizza, down by the docks in Ilwaco. Order their pepperoni pizza, and be sure to wear a bib, because your taste buds are going to crawl right out of your mouth and down onto the plate. I don't just like pizza, I *love* pizza, and we try a lot of pizza in the different places we visit. But I can tell you right now, I don't think I've ever had a pizza as good as the huge pie we enjoyed at

Meandering Down The Highway

Bubba's. Add to that the view of all the boats berthed right outside, and you just might never want to leave. My tastes are rather pedestrian, give me a pepperoni pizza every time. But if you prefer a little more variety, Bubba's offers all sorts of toppings to suit every palate, including shrimp, artichoke hearts, feta cheese, and linguisa, to name just a few. Whatever you order, I guarantee you'll be delighted.

Moving up the coast to Westport, we arrived in time to take in the 10th Annual Nautical Wood Sculpture Competition and see the tall ship *Lady Washington* arrive to berth near the *HMS Endeavour,* a replica of Captain Cook's ship that has toured the world representing the National Geographic Society. *Lady Washington* was built in Aberdeen to promote Grays Harbor, and depending on which of the locals you talk to, the project has been either a complete bust or a rousing success.

I've always loved Westport. I can spend hours wandering the docks looking at the commercial fishing boats, charter vessels and pleasure craft, watching people crabbing and fishing and the seagulls and pelicans foraging for their dinner, feeding the seals in the aquarium, or walking on the beach. Westport is a working fishing town, the Salmon Capitol of the World, and a laid back place that seems unchanged for the last 25 years.

One afternoon we were chatting with some folks and watching them check their crab traps when the *Lady Washington* headed out of the marina with a load of tourists for a three hour tour of the coast. As the ship made the turn near the fishing dock someone goofed, and the next thing we knew the wooden sailing ship had slammed into the dock, almost spilling all of us into the water. To add to the crew's embarrassment, part of the rigging caught on a piling supporting the dock, and by the time they got the bow untangled, the stem had swung around to bump the dock. Myself and a young fellow who had been crabbing had a great time throwing out good-natured jests, such as *"Can you say*

Meandering Down The Highway

tugboat?" and *"A three hour tour, huh? Didn't Gilligan's whole thing start out with a three hour tour too?"* By the time the ship got back underway, I suspect a few of the paying passengers would have been happy to give up their fares in return for just being allowed to get back on solid ground.

After three days at Pacific Aire RV Resort in Westport, we moved to the north side of Grays Harbor to spend a week at Ocean Mist Resort in Ocean City. I got a real shock when we drove into nearby Ocean Shores. When I lived in the area, Ocean Shores was just being discovered. In years past, I spent many happy hours digging razor clams on the beach, collecting driftwood or just enjoying watching the surf pound during winter storms. Today Ocean Shores has turned into a city, with upscale resorts and traffic congestion, and a casino under construction. Whatever Ocean Shores had that once drew me has been lost. If we hadn't already reserved our space on the north beach, we'd have turned around and gone back to Westport. But the folks at Ocean Mist made us feel welcome, and it made a convenient base for a few day trips in the area.

One of my favorite places on the Olympic Peninsula has always been Lake Quinault. The huge lake, on the western slope of the Olympic Mountains, is a beautiful spot, and anglers have pulled some monster fish out of the lake's waters. Miss Terry and I took a drive to the lake one day, pausing several times to check out interesting spots along the way. We wandered through historic Lake Quinault Lodge and the nearby General Store, then drove the loop road around the lake and into the back country.

The views of the Olympic Mountains, old homesteads, and the Olympic River were fantastic. This is still wild country - signs were up warning campers and hikers of an aggressive cougar in the area, and those who believe Sasquatch exists swear that this is the heart of Bigfoot country. Spend a few hours in this dense rain forest and you can understand how the mysterious creature could

Meandering Down The Highway

live here undiscovered. The Quinault Loop Road is about a 30 mile trip, part well maintained gravel road and part paved. The road is pretty narrow in places, definitely *not* a road to take your RV on. Leave it parked and drive your tow vehicle or dinghy. It's well worth your time to make the drive, the scenery is spectacular.

We've been enjoying very good weather since our trip started, for the most part. But we awoke to a hard rain falling on August 15. Since it was a Sunday, I went out for a newspaper and we spent the morning relaxing and catching up on what's been happening in the world. The rain increased all day, driven by a strong wind off the ocean, and several times wind gusts rocked our rig. We were glad we were snug inside and not out on the road heading somewhere. One of the nice things about the RV lifestyle is being able to have your home wherever you are. If the weather turns ugly, you can always park someplace and sit it out.

Monday morning, as we were preparing to head out from Ocean City, we discovered a large area of our carpeting, just behind the driver's seat, had been soaked. Apparently we've got a leak around the slide, which we suspect is due to the ill-fitting gasket. We dried the carpeting as best we could, and once again had dark thoughts about Fleetwood's quality control. Both Earnhardt's, where we purchased our RV, and Fleetwood, who manufactured it, have refused to fix the slide gaskets, which both have large gaps that allow drafts and insects into the RV when open. So much for quality control and buying a product with good name recognition.

We drove north on Highway 101, passing Humptulips, Lake Quinault, and Kalaloch, where we enjoyed spectacular views of the coastline. At Forks, we stopped to visit the Timber Museum, where displays illustrate the hard life of lumbermen in the dense forests of the Northwest woods. Lake Crescent is huge, and very beautiful. Several times we stopped to allow traffic to pass us and to take in the sights along the lake's shore.

Meandering Down The Highway

We had called Diamond Point Resort, in Sequim, to inquire about a space for a few days, and the young man I spoke to said to come on up, they had room and no reservation would be necessary. But when we arrived, a large woman with a surly attitude demanded to know what we wanted, and told us they were full. I pointed out that there were quite a few empty spaces and that we were both RPI and Coast to Coast members, but she insisted again that they were full. I've heard of some parks turning away Coast to Coast and RPI members, but this was the first time we had experienced it. Diamond Point is owned by K/M Resorts; a chain we would have another unpleasant experience with during our visit in Washington.

We drove another 25 miles or so to the Escapees Evergreen Coho Resort in Chimacum, arriving after the office closed, so we parked in the dry camp area for the night. Our reception at Evergreen Coho once again affirmed that becoming Escapees was one of the best moves we've made. The resort is beautiful and includes a great clubhouse, complete with game room, library and modem access. Everyone we met at the resort was friendly, as all of the Escapees are that we've met in our travels. We felt so comfortable there that we stayed ten days, using the resort as a base while we explored the area.

Another one of those quirky chance meetings happened while we were at Chimacum. Back in Mesa, Arizona, in May, we were in a Circuit City store with Miss Terry parents, helping them select a laptop computer when we got into a conversation with Fred Raphaely and his wife, also Escapees. Who should I encounter while checking my e-mail at the clubhouse in Chimacum but Fred! When you're an RVer on the road, it really is a small world.

Port Townsend, Washington is a town everyone should visit. The people are friendly, the waterfront area has excellent restaurants, neat shops, and the restored old buildings are

Meandering Down The Highway

beautiful. Port Townsend has quite a history; once a major shipping port, old time sea captains weren't hesitant to shanghai a man or two to round out their crews, and the rough and rowdy port was known for its saloons and shady ladies. The genteel folks lived up on the hill overlooking the waterfront, and today many of their Victorian homes have been refurbished, adding to the town's beauty. We attended a street fair and clambake while we were in Port Townsend, and those small town folks really made us feel welcome. We stopped for a pizza at one place, where the menu said their pizza was good for what ails you. I ordered the pizza that cures baldness and obesity, but it turns out that particular item wasn't on the menu. Darn the luck!

Okay, here's another tip for those of you who appreciate good food. The Chimacum Cafe, next door to the post office in Chimacum, has good food and great pie. After about the third or fourth person at the Escapee resort told us about the place, we decided we really needed to investigate, in the interest of good journalism, don't you know? Take my word for it, the next time you're in the area, stop in and give yourself a treat.

We made a day trip to Seattle, parking our truck in Bremerton and riding the ferry across Puget Sound. The waterfront district is a lot of fun, and Miss Terry really enjoyed Pike Place Public Market, where she stocked up on some goodies and we each bought a new pair of moccasin-style slippers for those cold evenings curled up with a good book back in the RV. We also visited Seattle Center and the Space Needle, but decided the $9 fare per person was more than we wanted to spend just to ride the elevator to the top. We walked from Pike Place to Seattle Center, but wised up and rode the monorail back. We did spend some time at the Imax Dome Theater and the Seattle Aquarium. I just love riding the ferries, watching the city's skyline, and the passing water craft. It was a long day, but a very good one, and when we finally crawled into bed back at our RV we were pleasantly

Meandering Down The Highway

exhausted.

As much as we liked Chimacum and the Port Townsend area, we eventually decided to see what else awaited us, and on Thursday, August 26 headed down the east side of the Olympic Peninsula, enjoying views of Dabob Bay and Hood Canal on one side and the Olympic Mountains on the other.

In Elma, we stayed at the Travel Inn, another K/M Resort. While they did give us a parking space with full hookups the first night and partial hookups for the remainder of our stay, we were really turned off when the fellow who checked us in made it clear to us he was doing us a favor, and ran down our home resort, telling us we should buy a membership from him instead. Those type of business tactics really upset me, and I made it a point to contact both RPI and Coast to Coast about the experience. The other folks in the office and the park were friendly, but given this experience, on top of our rude reception in Sequim, we won't be visiting any other K/M parks in the near future.

When we came through Grays Harbor the first time, my friends Buddy and Faye Bosarge were up in Alaska. Buddy is a taxidermist, and spends the summer working in Alaska. They were back, but out crabbing at Westport. I saw the opportunity for a free meal there, so we drove out to Westport to catch up with our friends on the dock. We had a good reunion, with lots of hugs and backslapping, and by then Buddy had caught enough Dungeness and Red Rock crabs to feed me, so we drove back to their place in Hoquiam for dinner. The secret to successful fulltime RVing is to know where you can scrounge a free meal here and there. It really stretches the budget, not to mention the waistline.

With the Labor Day holiday coming up, we needed to get off the road and finish work on this issue of the newspaper. Several Coast to Coast and RPI campgrounds we looked into told us they only accepted members from their home park over the holiday, but the nice folks at Western Horizon's Ocean Shores Resort

Meandering Down The Highway

made us feel welcome. This is a great park, every space is bordered by trees or hedges to give you a sense of privacy, and I plan on spending some time in the spa while we're here.

As we wrap up this issue of the *Gypsy Journal,* a nice breeze is blowing and the sky is blue, with just a few high clouds. Kids are laughing and playing outside and we're snug and happy inside our house on wheels. We've been on the road over two months now. We've covered a lot of territory, from Arizona through New Mexico, and Colorado to Wyoming, on through Montana to Idaho, into Oregon and here to the beaches of Washington. In fact, we've covered too much territory. We need to slow our pace down a little bit, stop and smell the roses along the way. Someone asked us just the other day if we had any regrets in making the move from a conventional lifestyle to the life of fulltimers on the road. Our only regret is that we didn't do it sooner. Our stress level has dropped to almost nothing, we sleep better than we ever did before, and each new day is an adventure. It's the greatest life there is and we'd never go back to our old workaholic ways. There's a big old country out there, full of wonderful places to explore and people to meet, and we plan to see it all. Next issue we'll have more adventures to share as we see more of this wonderful country of ours. Until then, hope to see you in our travels.

Meandering Down The Highway

November-December, 1999

We loved our time on the Olympic Peninsula, but with Labor Day behind us, the chill in the air let us know it was time to turn the nose of our rig southward in search of warmer temperatures and new adventures. We had a great summer along the coast, but new adventures await us down the road.

We left Ocean Shores Resort in Ocean City, Washington September 9 and drove to Longview, where we finally caught up with our friends Don and Linda Bonahom. When we came through Longview a few weeks earlier, we discovered that Don and his family were in Montana, recovering from a nasty automobile accident. Fortunately they were all wearing seat belts, and though their Suburban was totaled when a truck crossed the center line and hit them, they came away from the experience bruised and battered, but alive. I have to admit, I never used to wear my seat belt regularly, but after seeing photographs of Don's truck, I'm a believer. The huge front end of the Suburban was so crushed that it looked like a van. That extra second or two that it took to put on their seat belts saved our friends' lives.

After our reunion, we drove on to Portland, where we had reservations at the gun show in the Expo Center. Jantzen Beach RV Park was nice, though working our table at the gun show kept us from spending much time at the park. The only complaint I have about Jantzen Beach is the noise from the big airplanes coming in for a landing at Portland's airport. I swear a couple of times I could have reached up and snatched a bag of those salted peanuts the flight attendants were passing out.

Meandering Down The Highway

We had been having some problems with backfiring, and our fuel economy (not that *any* RV is economical to drive) had really dropped since we left Arizona. I suspected a problem with our Banks exhaust system, possibly an air leak. Camping World in Wilsonville, just south of Portland, was kind enough to squeeze us in to check out the problem. They discovered a spark plug heat shield that was shorting out a plug wire and remedied the problem. Since the work was completed late in the day, we spent Monday night, September 13, dry camping in their parking lot. The *Gypsy Journal* is quickly developing a following - when we pulled into Camping World, a young fellow stopped Miss Terry to tell her he had read the first issue and asked for a copy of the latest paper.

Back To The Coast

Tuesday morning we drove back to Newport, on the Oregon coast, to drive the southern portion of Highway 101 that we had missed earlier. We stopped at the Wal-Mart in Woodburn and fell in love. There was one of those traveling RV shows, where a dealer sets up a few units in a parking lot, so after our shopping was completed, we walked over to have a look. I've never thought I'd want a diesel rig, but we stepped inside a 40 foot Gulf Stream Tour Master and all that changed. We're talking the ultimate in luxury here, people. A Jacuzzi bathtub, walk in cedar closet, tons of storage space inside the unit, and all of that beautiful basement storage down below. Not to mention the power to tame the biggest hills. Shoot, if Miss Terry ever got tired of my foolishness, I could just go sleep in the basement compartment for a day or two.

Of course, we realize that a rig like that's way out of our price range, but I've always believed that where there's a will, there's a way. I'm thinking about getting myself a cardboard sign that says "*Will Work For RV*" or something like that, and hanging out on the street corners at some of the fancier RV resorts. How about

Meandering Down The Highway

"Homeless In A Pace Arrow, Please Help"? That should jar the sympathies of some of those high line motorcoach owners, don't you think? Heck, if it works out, I may get myself another sign and see if we can't step up from our Toyota pickup into a Ford Expedition or something like that.

Climbing through the hills toward the coast, the engine backfired once, so we're still not sure if we've solved the problem. It was in the low 90s near Portland, but by the time we were back on the coast, the temperature had dropped to the 50s, giving us a real chill.

In several places in Oregon we saw signs warning that drunk drivers will forfeit their vehicles. I don't think that's a bad idea at all, given the high death rate from alcohol related accidents.

We tried to get into Whalers Rest, a Coast to Coast park in Newport, but they were full, so we drove on to Florence, where the RPI affiliate turned us away because we didn't have a reservation. We're finding that traveling as we do, trying not to maintain too tight a schedule, has its drawbacks, including making it hard to take advantage of our campground memberships. We got into this lifestyle to have as much freedom as possible, and we're trying to avoid the restrictions imposed by reservations and schedules as much as we can. But freedom always comes with a price. Looking in our Passport America guidebook, we discovered Lakeshore RV Park in Florence, where Jim and Becky Lupton made room for us even though it was late in the day and we didn't have reservations.

The drive through the Cape Perpetua area is astounding, but take it slow and easy, there are a lot of curves. We stopped at a viewpoint just north of Sea Lion Caves to take some pictures of the sea lions sunning themselves on the rocks below and of the Heceta Head Lighthouse. A car pulled up and a nice looking young couple got out to admire the view. It turns out the young man is terribly afraid of heights - he stopped about ten feet from

Meandering Down The Highway

the rock wall, squatted down and duck-walked to the wall, where he cautiously peered over the edge, then drew his head back quickly. He finally worked up his courage and stood up, asking if it was okay if he leaned on me. I've got my own phobias, including some concerns about high places, so I was happy to oblige. My young friend dug his fingers into my shoulder, took one good long look, and was satisfied. Dropping back to his crouch, he thanked me and scooted back to a comfortable distance, then returned to his car.

We spent a couple of days exploring Florence. One interesting sight was the Darlingtonia Botanical Gardens, where a path leads through the forest a short distance to a bog where weird carnivorous plants grow wild. Like something out of a science fiction movie, the plants lure insects into their petals, where they become disoriented and are trapped. The plant then digests the unlucky intruder. I like to think of it as nature's way of getting back at all of you vegetarians out there.

The Oregon Dunes National Recreation Area starts in Florence, and offers miles of hiking. Local concessionaires offer horse rentals or you can rent a sand buggy to explore the dunes.

Break Down

We've decided our Pace Arrow Vision motorhome is aptly named - when you first see it, you have a vision of a top of the line motorcoach. But all it really is is a mirage. Repeated problems with quality control have convinced us that the vision is false. From light fixtures that self-destruct, to a shower stall that was so poorly caulked that it leaked terribly, to slide-out gaskets so ill-fitted that every insect within miles comes in at night, not to mention an oven whose gaskets crumbled before we ever used the unit, we smell the distinct aroma of a lemon. Our dissatisfaction increased in Florence, when we noticed our living room slide-out was coming out two or three inches as we drove down the highway. Investigation showed the ram that controls the slide-out

Meandering Down The Highway

was pouring hydraulic fluid. I called Fleetwood, and though they wouldn't cover the repair cost, the customer service department put me on hold for a few minutes, then returned to tell me they had made an appointment for us at Porter's RV & Marine in Coos Bay. The drive from Florence to Coos Bay is about 50 miles, so we jury-rigged a couple of travel rods and headed for our appointment, worrying all the way.

Mike Arsenault and Brandi Allen at Porter's were wonderful to us, diagnosing the problem, getting on the telephone to Fleetwood to arrange to have the part overnight expressed in, and calling the nearby Lucky Logger RV Park to reserve a space for us. When you're stuck on the road somewhere far from familiar faces, service like we received from Porter's is really a comfort. We arrived in Coos Bay on Thursday afternoon, the ram arrived about noon on Friday, and by 3 p.m. Mike had us back on the road. Porter's is a shop we can recommend completely. Mike, Brandi and everyone else was very friendly and helpful. We've heard some real horror stories about RV repair shops around the country, but Porter's really took good care of us.

Before the slide-out problem developed, we had arranged for Escapees Mail Service to forward our mail to Brookings, Oregon, about 100 miles south of Coos Bay, assuming we'd be there on Thursday or Friday to pick it up. When we learned we'd be delayed awaiting repairs, Mike at Porter's called the Brookings Post Office to learn they were closed on Saturdays. After parking the RV at Lucky Logger, Miss Terry and I decided to drive on down to Brookings to retrieve our mail, so we wouldn't have to wait until after the weekend to get it.

The drive down the coast was spectacular - it was one of those rare days along the Oregon coast when the sun is shining brightly and there's not a cloud in the sky. The rock formations along the coast were awesome, and we took advantage of several pullouts to stop and drink in the scenery. Along this stretch of

Meandering Down The Highway

highway is the Damas Creek Bridge, which at 345 feet high, is the highest bridge in Oregon

On the return trip we stopped at the Bandon Cheese Company, where we sampled some of their many varieties of cheeses and bought some goodies and ice cream cones. Here's a tip for you - if you enjoy cheese, try the smoked cheddar. We purchased a couple of packages and combined with crackers, it really makes a great snack during the middle of the day.

Efforts were still ongoing to dismantle the stern of the *New Carissa,* which broke up off Coos Bay, spilling 55,000 gallons of oil into the water, creating a hazard to the fragile coastal environment and to marine traffic. Heavy waves were making it hazardous for the workers, who were in a race against time to get the wreck dismantled and towed out to deeper water to sink before winter sets in. One enterprising local company was offering rides out along the dunes to view the shipwreck, making the best of a bad situation. Cleanup efforts have been mostly successful and the coast has been spared the terrible damage the Alaskan environment suffered when the *Exxon Valdez* wrecked a few years ago.

When we left Coos Bay Saturday morning with our repairs completed, we were glad we made our trip to Brookings to pick up our mail earlier in the week - the fog had closed in and on this trip down the coast visibility was just about nil. It was a surreal experience driving along the coast with the thick fog blanketing everything and just the tips of the largest rock formations poking through. Miss Terry said it was like driving through cotton candy.

On To California

Crossing into California, we stopped at the port of entry to swear we weren't carrying any illegal produce, nuclear weapons or undocumented aliens, and picked up a souvenir road map that contained several discount coupons for state attractions. The drive down Highway 101 through the California redwoods is a

Meandering Down The Highway

trip everyone should make. Those giant trees, 300 feet or more high, have to be seen to be believed. We stopped at the Redwoods National Park Information Center in Crescent City, where we purchased a Golden Eagle Pass, allowing us entrance to National Parks and Monuments and other sites administered by the Parks Service. At $50 for a family unit, the pass is a good bargain - we've spent nearly that much in admission fees in the last three months.

Just outside of Crescent City I saw a sign urging us to visit a shark petting tank. When I was a teenager, I learned you don't have to pet to be popular. I think that's especially true when it comes to sharks. I saw the movie *Jaws*. If I want to get close up and personal with a shark, all I have to do is invite my ex-wife's attorney to lunch.

As soon as you enter California from Oregon, you see an increase in agricultural activity, with lots of fields and irrigation going on. Smith River bills itself as the Easter Lily Capital of the World, and huge commercial farms produce thousands of plants every year.

Soon after it enters California, Highway 101 loses its character and becomes just another four lane highway for a distance, then reverts back to a winding two lane road as you enter the redwood country, where it becomes known as the Redwood Highway. At Brookings, Oregon we paid $1.53 a gallon for gasoline, and wondered if we should have waited until we were in California to fuel up. As it turned out, we were glad we did, when we saw California gas advertised at $1.69.

We arrived at Klamath River RV Park, just south of Klamath, about 5 p.m. Just in time to park, hook up to water and electric, then head over to the club house for the ice cream social. Jim and Cathie Brubaker, from Yreka, California were celebrating Cathie's birthday, so everyone joined in singing *Happy Birthday* to her. We had met the Brubaker's at the Life on Wheels

Meandering Down The Highway

Conference in Idaho in July, so it was nice to cross their path again.

Klamath River is a neat place, situated right on the river's edge about two miles inland from the coast. The park has a boat dock, and we wandered down to check out the action just in time to see Gary Hopkins land a huge salmon. We also watched three seals doing some fishing themselves, much to the chagrin of the human fishermen, who don't appreciate losing trophy fish to the competition. Gary and his pretty wife Tina are from Mesa, Arizona and spend several months of every year on the road pulling their Airstream trailer, chasing the best fishing opportunities and exploring. They and several other couples meet at Klamath River RV Park every year for the salmon fishing and the scenery, and people were so nice that we'll be going back too. Managers Bobby and Leslie Cano, along with their assistant, Lesley Boardman, really made us feel welcome and a part of the family.

This is wild country - the park closes from November through April of every year due to high water and bad weather, and they had to install an electric device on the trash containers to shock the local bears out of dumpster diving. If you're looking for a park where you'll be pampered with jacuzzis, big screen televisions, tennis courts and heated swimming pools, keep on driving. But if your priorities lie more in the direction of friendly people, natural beauty and the great outdoors, I think you'll like Klamath River RV Park.

We would have loved to linger longer at Klamath River, but we needed to be in southern California by the end of the week and wanted to do some exploring on the way. So Sunday morning we hit the road again, headed south through the great trees. Just south of Orick, at Freshwater Lagoon, dozens of RVers were dry camping alongside the highway near the beach. The boondocking area, administered by the State of California, has portable toilets

Meandering Down The Highway

and trash dumpsters, and spectacular scenery. There is a small daily fee, on the honor system, and we made a mental note to add it to the list of places we'll be returning to. There wasn't much in the way of amenities, but with the Pacific Ocean at your doorstep, what more do you need?

At Orick, several shops and stands along the highway sell redwood burls and other redwood souvenirs. A Corvette club was pulled off at a gas station, and for just a moment or two I missed my vintage Corvette back in Arizona, but then realized I wouldn't trade our life on the road for all the classic cars in the world.

At the Redwood Trails RV Resort, cars and RVs were lined up along the highway watching a huge herd of elk browse in a meadow. A nearby sign identified it as the world's largest Roosevelt elk herd. There was one magnificent bull, three or four smaller spike bulls and lots of cows ands yearlings. Miss Terry counted the legs and divided by four, coming up with 65 elk, more or less. Wildlife has a frustrating way of moving around when you want them to stand still to be counted. The big old bull bugled several times, a sound that will send a thrill right through you. Everyone was taking pictures and pointing video cameras their way, and of course one jerk had to pick up a rock and fling it at the bull to get his attention. The slob got everyone else's attention too, and several people yelled at him for his boorish manners. Some people are among the dumbest animals I've ever seen.

Driving by the Eel River Sawmill, we saw piles of logs stacked two and three stories high that seemed to go on forever. Log cabins in waiting.

We detoured off Highway 101 to take the 32 mile drive down the Avenue of the Giants, one of the most memorable stretches of road we've ever traveled. The road gets a bit narrow and has its share of twists and turns, but there are plenty of pullouts and even the biggest RV can make the trip with just a little bit of care. Driving down the road, with the towering trees almost close

Meandering Down The Highway

enough to reach out and touch was like driving through the world's longest and most scenic tunnel - a tunnel of ancient trees that stretches hundreds of feet into the clouds.

I'm always amazed how many people drive through such scenic wonders at high speeds, never pausing a minute to see all of the beauty around them. It's like they have a giant list of places to visit and not enough time to do it in, so they go everywhere and never slow down long enough to see anything. I'm always happy to pull over and let those kinds of drivers get on down the road while we enjoy the countryside.

We learned an important lesson about being flexible, and the neat places hiding off the beaten path waiting to be discovered. It was getting late in the day, and we began looking for a place to stop for the night. Our Passport America book listed BJ Walls Campground in Nice, so we turned off down State Highway 20, a narrow twisting road that took us east. We didn't check our road map and therefore didn't realize how far Nice was from Highway 101 until it was too late to turn back, which is a good thing, or we wouldn't have found Clear Lake and the tiny community of Nice (pronounced neese).

Clear Lake is huge, the largest natural lake in California. The folks at the campground were all very friendly, and even though our rig was really too big for the place, a couple of helpful fellows got us parked, and back out again the next morning. BJ Walls has its own pier and a great little restaurant that everyone raved about. The local fishermen tell me that the bass and catfish in Clear Lake provide plenty of action, and we just missed a seaplane fly-in that I would have loved to be on hand to see.

Monday morning we were headed out of town when we discovered the Featherbed Railroad Company, a bed and breakfast that uses old railroad cabooses as guest cottages. We just had to stop and check the place out. A woman poked her head out of one of the cabooses to tell us that this was her third year

Meandering Down The Highway

visiting and that she loved the place. It's no wonder, we were ready to park the RV and check in for a day or two ourselves. A sign in the parking lot read For Lovers Only. If you're looking for a romantic vacation or getaway for a honeymoon, anniversary or just because, check out the Featherbed Railroad Company in Nice. It's one of the most unique sights we've come across in our travels.

    A sign as we entered Lucerne called the town the Switzerland of America. We couldn't see any connection. Not an Alp, nor even a bit of Swiss chocolate in sight. Maybe they eat a lot of cheese in Lucerne, I don't know. We followed Highway 20 east for another 50 winding, narrow miles or so until we came to Interstate 5. I'm usually not a fan of the superslabs, but after all of the hairpin turns we'd just been on, that big old wide highway was a welcome sight. Forgetting all I've said about slowing down and smelling the roses along the way, I edged the speedometer up to about 60 and steered the RV south toward Sacramento.

    Gassing up in Sacramento, our mileage was 5.89 miles per gallon, still a long way from the 7 plus mpg we enjoyed earlier in our trip. Drivers of other Pace Arrows with the 460 Ford engines tell me they're getting much better mileage, and we're still not sure why ours is so bad. We dropped several sample bundles of newspapers off at the Camping World in Sacramento, then returned to the Interstate, still driving south. It was about 3 p.m. and traffic was getting heavy, but moving along very well.

    About 7 p.m. we arrived at Sommerville's Almond Tree RV Park near Coalinga. The office was closed, so we dropped our fee into the night slot and found a site. It was hot, and we needed a treat, so we changed into swimsuits and headed for the pool. The water was cold getting in, but after just a moment or two it really felt good.

    Cooled down and dried off, we were back in the RV when someone came calling, a nice couple from southern California

Meandering Down The Highway

who had picked up a *Gypsy Journal* in Portland. They spotted our pickup and wanted to introduce themselves. We chatted for a while, and after our guests left ate a quick dinner and went to bed.

Early the next morning I woke up to the sounds of someone moving around outside the RV. Thinking it was one of our neighbors getting ready to pull out, I closed my eyes and tried to get back to sleep, but something just didn't feel right. Getting up, I peeked outside to see a young man standing near our door, and another at the back of the rig. Both were wearing orange T-shirts, and I learned later they may have been part of a construction crew working on a nearby road project and staying in the campground.. They saw me and took off in a hurry, so I went outside to check things out. One of the pins that secure our Toyota pickup to the tow bar was lying on the ground and the truck was unlocked. I'm convinced if I had ignored that little nagging worry, we would have awakened to find our truck stolen. Within moments we were unhooked and back on the road. I have to say in defense of the RV park that when I called them later to report what happened, the lady I talked to was very apologetic and quick to promise she would investigate. The world we live in isn't perfect, and no matter where you are, you have to be alert to those who would take advantage of you. But overall, we've found our fulltime RV lifestyle to be much safer than living in a city. In thousands of miles of traveling, this is the first time we've run into any trouble.

Fun On The Beach

State Highway 198 west from Coalinga to Highway 101 is another snarl of hairpin curves and steep hills, not really suited to a big RV. But there was no traffic to speak of, the morning was gorgeous, and we spotted quite a bit of wildlife, including deer, prairie dogs and a coyote loping across a field.

Okay, I know someone out there is reading this and asking why we left Highway 101, drove east on a narrow two lane road to drive south on the interstate, then back west to 101 on another

Meandering Down The Highway

secondary road. Well... because it was there. Actually, we wanted to avoid the San Francisco area this trip, but we did want to get back to the coast for a visit to the Morro Bay and Pismo Beach area. That why it's called *meandering* down the highway. Anyone can drive from point A to point B.

There's a Coast to Coast park in Avila, near Pismo Beach, but our RV is too long, so we arranged for a three night stay at Silver Spur RV Park in Oceano. Situated on the edge of the dunes of the Oceano Dunes State Vehicular Recreation Area about 3/4 mile from the beach, Silver Spur also has stables with horses for rent. They advertise that they are modem friendly, but it turns out that the only modem hookup is on an outside pay telephone, with a flimsy table that I wouldn't trust to hold a pocket calculator, let alone an expensive laptop computer. Not that it matters, it's impossible to see the computer screen standing outdoors anyway. I hadn't had the chance to check my e-mail in several days, so it was a real disappointment. As portable computers become more and more important to the RVing public, I think the parks who don't make some accommodation for getting online will be left in the dust. I realize that the cost of installing dedicated telephone lines to every site is out of reach for most smaller parks, but any RV park that can't make a plug-in available somewhere for their customers doesn't rate very high in my book.

Greater minds than the tiny one that resides in my bald head have pondered whether reincarnation is fact or fantasy, but if our spirits *do* return to live again, remind me to spend one of my lives in Morro Bay, California. (Miss Terry warns me to be careful what I wish for. If reincarnation *is* real, she thinks with my luck, I'll come back as a seagull. I can live with that - there are a few folks I know that I'd love to get even with!) I first discovered this little fishing town, with its monolith rock guarding the bay, over 20 years ago. I returned with Miss Terry on our honeymoon a couple of years ago and was thrilled to find it largely unchanged.

Meandering Down The Highway

The fishing boats still return after their trips out to sea, the people are still friendly and the pace is still just a bit slower.

One real treat for me are the delicious cinnamon rolls they serve at Crills II on the Embarcadero, and I've been nagging Miss Terry for months to take me back to the bay so I can stuff myself on them. Wednesday morning we left the RV and drove the thirty miles or so up to Morro Bay, where the nice young lady behind the counter at Crills served up a huge roll, dripping with caramel and nuts. A light rain was falling, but we took our treats outside under the canopy to eat. The Embarcadero stretches along Morro Bay's waterfront, with an aquarium, several restaurants and all sorts of specialty shops that are fun to browse through. We spent the morning wandering around and drinking in all of the sights along the waterfront. The sky opened up and the rain began to pour furiously, so we reluctantly climbed back in the truck and went back to our RV, promising ourselves we'll return when we have more time.

Pismo Beach is another favorite of mine. I can waste hours on the pier there, watching the youngsters surfing, the fishermen trying to hook supper, and the seagulls and pelicans begging for handouts. Lately the sea otters have been taking a big toll on Pismo Beach's clams, but in years past it's been a good place to dig for delicious shellfish.

We stopped at the Pierside Restaurant for dinner twice while we were in Pismo Beach, and I can really recommend their Captain's Combo. You can't walk away from the table hungry, the portions are huge.

Moving On

After a few days in Oceano, we headed south on Highway 101 through Santa Barbara and Ventura to hook up with Interstate 5, then turned onto Highway 14 to Lancaster. I was apprehensive about driving the rig through the outskirts of the Los Angeles metropolitan area, but even though traffic was heavy for a few

Meandering Down The Highway

miles as we neared Los Angeles, we got through just fine. At times like this, I really appreciate having a co-pilot like Miss Terry to alert me to cars merging into my lane from the right and help keep an eye ahead for changing traffic conditions.

We have several little ventures going to help cover our expenses, including selling handgun grips at gun shows in the towns we visit. The gun show scheduled for Lancaster, California was a big success for us. We did a steady business all day long both days of the show, and met some nice people.

I'm always fascinated by the people we run into again and again as we travel, or who have some connection to other people we've met. Such was the case in Lancaster. Shortly after we got set up in the RV park at the fairgrounds, a rig pulled in beside us and we wandered over to get acquainted. Ken Weisner and his wife Jean, from Apple Valley, California were selling beef jerky at the show. We got to talking and mentioned our old hometown back in Arizona's White Mountains. Ken told us that he and his son, who lives in Tucson, had been fishing in the White Mountains a year or so ago when a newspaper reporter took their photograph and printed it in the newspaper. Imagine our mutual surprise when I learned that and told Ken I had owned that very newspaper and it was one of my reporters who took the photo! That small world thing kicking in again. But the story doesn't end there, a little more conversation and we discovered that we had met Ken's son, also named Ken, at a gun show in Tucson back in May!

We left Lancaster about 5 p.m. on Sunday afternoon, September 26 and made the short drive west to Gorman, on Interstate 5, and Western Horizon's Pyramid Lake Resort. After the friendly reception we received at Western Horizon's Ocean Shores Resort, we decided to join the Western Horizon system. We received the same warm welcome at Pyramid Lake as we did at Ocean Shores, and quickly got settled in for a three day visit.

Meandering Down The Highway

Only an hour north of Los Angeles, Pyramid Lake made a good base for our time in the area. One day we drove south to Newhall to drop off some newspapers at the Camping World store there and a visit with manager Mark Lowrey. The weird small world syndrome happened again - later we stopped to do some grocery shopping at a supermarket in Valencia and got to talking to the cashier. When we mentioned we were fulltime RVers, she told us we should stop at Camping World and meet her son-in-law, Mark, the very person we had just left. Every night at Pyramid Lake the local coyotes sang us to sleep.

One thing that really stood out during our time at Pyramid Lake Resort was getting our mail. We had left instructions for our mail forwarding service to send our mail in care of General Delivery to the post office in Gorman. This is the accepted way for fulltimers to get their mail. You choose a town on your planned route, call your mail forwarding service, tell them where you want your mail sent, and it's usually waiting for you when you arrive. Usually the local post office isn't hard to find, especially in the small towns we prefer. We just look for a flagpole a block or so off the main highway - it's either the post office or the police station. If it's the latter, they can always direct us to the right place. But in Gorman, we couldn't find the post office, though the place is tiny, not much more than a couple of restaurants and gas stations. Finally I inquired at a garage and was directed to the local liquor store. Not sure I was in the right place, I went on in. I still wasn't sure I had found the post office - there was a good supply of liquor, and a couple of big boxes of X-rated videos for sale on the counter, but not a postage stamp or automatic weapon to be seen. But sure enough, they had a corner of the store designated as the local United States post office, and there was our mail.

While we were at Pyramid Lake we met Ed and Gloria

Meandering Down The Highway

Helmuth, seminar coordinators for the Escapees Club Spring Escapade. They had picked up a copy of the *Gypsy Journal* and asked if I might be interested in teaching a class or two at the Escapade in Lancaster in April of next year. I'm not much of a public speaker, and the thought of standing up in front of a large group of people and talking makes my stomach turn cartwheels. But Gloria assures me I'll do fine, so we'll see. We left it with me promising to consider teaching a seminar on baby boomer RVers and another on working on the road. Miss Terry is encouraging me to teach the classes, but I think that's just because she gets a real thrill out of watching me step on my tongue from time to time.

We spent one day visiting my sister Maggie McCormack and her husband Mac in Bakersfield. Maggie and I don't get to see as much of each other as we'd like to, but it's always nice to visit. She and Mac always make us feel welcome and put on a big feed whenever we visit. While we were in Bakersfield, we managed to drop off a bundle of sample newspapers in the local Camping World store. The Bakersfield Camping World is a tiny operation in comparison to their other stores that we've visited, but the folks working there were just as friendly as we've come to expect from Camping World employees.

Bakersfield is the hometown of country music star Buck Owens, and Miss Terry has fond memories of hearing the singer perform at an Air Force base in Puerto Rico when she was a youngster and her father was still in the service. We stopped for a visit at Buck Owens' Crystal Palace dinner theater and museum in Bakersfield, where there is a nice collection of mementos from his career and a gift shop offering everything from country music and gifts to souvenirs. The museum is surrounded by a boardwalk lined with storefront windows filled with memorabilia of Owens and other country music stars. The theater is equipped with state

Meandering Down The Highway

of the art sound and lighting equipment and giant video screens, and has a huge dance floor. Maggie tells me the singer makes frequent appearances at the club and contributes a lot to the betterment of his community, but we missed him this trip. Hopefully we can catch his show another time when we visit.

Wednesday morning, September 29, we left Pyramid Lake and pointed the nose of the RV east toward Arizona. We stopped and spent a couple of hours wandering through the 20 Mule Team Museum in Boron, California. The small town museum has a nice collection of local historical artifacts, as well as displays on the borax industry that has thrived in the area for a century.

At Barstow, we took a detour to visit the ghost town of Calico, now restored as a tourist site. Miss Terry and I are both history nuts, so we enjoyed roaming through the old buildings and looking at all of the things on display. If you can get past the costumed gunfighters and souvenir stands, Calico has a lot of history to it.

Back Home In Arizona

My buddy Mike Howard in Kingman, Arizona must be getting tired of us visiting. When Miss Terry and I stopped by last spring, we both came down with a nasty bug and spent several days moaning and groaning until we got to feeling well enough to head home. The day after we left, Mike came down with the flu. This trip I began sneezing and my head clogged up as soon as we got to town. I thought it was just allergies, but then Miss Terry started showing symptoms of a cold too. Poor Mike tried to keep smiling, but by the time we left, he was complaining of a sore throat and headache too. When I spoke to him a few days later, he was really sick. Hey, if you can't share with your friends, who can you share with?

We worked the gun show in Kingman, which was a total bust, but we spent five nights parked in Mike's driveway and had

Meandering Down The Highway

a good reunion. Mike liked our RV and by the time we were ready to leave, he was saying (between sneezes) that he could live full time in one of these rigs too. I don't think he was really serious, he just wants to be mobile enough to avoid us when we get to feeling puny and need a place to crash.

We had some business to take care of in Arizona, so we made reservations at Western Horizon's Verde River Recreational Resort in Camp Verde for a few days. I think the Verde River Resort may well be my favorite of all of the parks we've visited so far. High enough from the desert to be comfortable, yet close enough to Phoenix, Flagstaff and Prescott to be convenient, we plan to use the resort whenever we stop into Arizona to visit family and friends. The park features a club house, huge swimming pool, hot tub, level grassy sites and a friendly staff.

There is a lot to see and do in the Verde Valley, but since we covered the area in our first issue, we won't go over old ground here. Just let me say that if you are going to be spending some time in Arizona, plan to visit the Verde Valley for a few days. I think you'll find it will be well worth your time.

More small world syndrome - when we were staying at Ocean Shores Resort in Washington, Mel and Jeanette Gray were parked next to us for a week or so. We barely got the rig hooked up at Verde River before Mel stopped in to say hello. They had arrived a few days ahead of us and were parked a few spaces away.

Never underestimate the power of positive sniveling. Within a few days of the repairs to our living room slide, the bedroom slide in our motorhome began showing the same symptoms, the bottom slipping out two inches or so while we drive down the highway. Apparently something in the design of the rear slide keeps it from coming out as far on its own as the big living room slide, because the repair facilities I spoke to all assured me it wouldn't come out any further while in transit. But I was fed up,

Meandering Down The Highway

and when I called Fleetwood to complain, I refused to hang up until I got to someone high enough up the pecking order to do us some good.

When I listed all of the things wrong with the motorhome, the customer service department representative agreed there were some serious problems that needed attention, and made arrangements for us to go to a Fleetwood repair facility, Acacia RV, in Colton, California, just down the highway from the factory in Riverside. I called Steve at Acacia RV and he scheduled us for a full day in the shop on October 20. Since Acacia is only a few miles from the Fleetwood factory in Riverside, Steve said arrangements had been made for his shop to pick up anything needed to get the work done. A call back to Fleetwood confirmed that we'd be able to get everything handled to our satisfaction. Hopefully we'll finally get the rig up to standard.

We stayed at Verde River a week, then moved down to Mesa, Arizona to park in the driveway of Miss Terry's grandmother's house for several days while we visited my son and Terry's family, and wrapped up some business and tried to reduce some of the things we still had in a storage locker by having a yard sale. We're amazed at how much money we've taken in on things we no longer need or want, and as we travel we find that we don't miss most of the "stuff" that tied us down to our old lifestyle. We've come to realize that most people spend their lives working to acquire all of the latest goodies Madison Avenue convinces us we must have to be worthy human beings, only to find their expensive toys outdated when the next year's model hits the streets. Since we made the decision to stop being slaves to material things, our lives are simpler and much more relaxed.

We've had many people tell us they'd like to travel fulltime, but they're just not willing to part with everything they own. I can understand that, we felt the same way for years. But one day we

Meandering Down The Highway

looked around ourselves, at our big house, with its deck and hot tub and the garage holding our four classic cars, and realized that with our heavy work schedules, we hadn't taken the old cars to a car show in over a year, and it had been nearly a month since we'd found the time to soak in the hot tub. We were too busy working to support our toys to have the time to enjoy them.

Now we live at a slower pace - most mornings we peek out at the world with one bleary eye, then roll over and snooze another half hour or so before we get up. We open our window blinds, and depending on what part of the country we're in, we might be greeted with spectacular mountain scenery, the sound of surf crashing on a beach, or a desert vista. In the evening we sit outside under our awning visiting with friendly neighbors or just enjoying quiet time alone. When it's getting late, but we're absorbed in a good book, we don't have to put it down and get to sleep to make it to an early morning meeting - we make our own schedules. Everything we need or want is right inside our motorhome, and we've finally got the time to enjoy each other and to see all of the places we've always wanted to visit. We've dined on fresh seafood that was swimming in the ocean only a few hours earlier, picked wild blackberries to top our morning pancakes, and strolled miles of wild beaches. We've spotted an interesting roadside scene and stopped to investigate at our leisure, and we've had the freedom to spend weeks in places we enjoy, not having to cram everything into a few days like the work weary vacationers we've seen. To us, that's a pretty good tradeoff for a houseful of dusty treasures we never had the time to enjoy anyway.

Add to that the health benefits. I'd been having some heart problems in our old high pressure life, and neither of us slept well. With so much less stress in our lives, now we both feel great. I think there were two real wake up calls for us that helped us arrive at the decision to go fulltime. We had several friends in their 40s

Meandering Down The Highway

die suddenly, all of them living stressful lives. When you're younger and know you're invincible, the prospect of dying is impossible to conceive. But as your peers begin to fall, you suddenly realize it *can* happen to you.

I think the final straw for us came in the summer of 1998. I was driving a step van carrying four 1500 pound rolls of newsprint for our newspaper when someone ran a traffic light in front of me. I managed to stomp on the brakes and avoid a collision, but the load came loose and slammed into me, pinning me between a couple of tons of newsprint and the steering wheel and dashboard. The force of the impact was enough to bend the steering wheel nearly in half, completely straighten the steel frame of my seat, and left me trapped and unable to breathe due to the crushing weight on top of me. To this day I don't know how I did it, but I finally managed to pull myself out of the truck and fell into the roadway.

I came through the experience with some pretty well torn up insides, and enough bruises to make you think I'd gone a few rounds in the ring with Mohamad Ali. To make a bad situation even worse, someone saw the ambulance attendants working on me in the street and called Miss Terry to tell her I'd been killed in an accident. By the time the poor lady made it to the emergency room of the hospital and learned I was somewhat battered, but definitely alive, she was understandably a basket case. I'd already survived a few years playing soldier, a couple of nasty automobile crashes and a heart attack. One begins to wonder how many times you can roll the dice. I've always believed I'll live forever, since heaven won't let me in and the devil's afraid I'll try to take over, but why not spend your life having fun instead of working yourself into an early grave? There's more to life than long hours, difficult customers, unappreciative employees and taxes. I've never regretted changing lifestyles, and Miss Terry and I are in

Meandering Down The Highway

agreement that we'd never go back to our old way of living and working.

The weather in Mesa wasn't as hot as it was when we were there in June, but the thermometer climbed over 100 every day, though the nights cooled off nicely. While we were in the Mesa area, we took a day trip south to Casa Grande to visit two RV parks, the Escapee Club's Rovers Roost and Western Horizon's Desert Shadows RV Resort. Casa Grande is popular with snowbird RVers who migrate south in the winter to escape the cold weather up north and in the Midwest. Desert Shadows doesn't have the visual appeal that the other Western Horizon resorts we've visited have, but admittedly we don't like the desert all that much. But the resort has a huge clubhouse, pool and an exercise room. Everyone was friendly and made us feel welcome. The woman in the office at Rovers Roost, like any Escapees park, was friendly and outgoing. We don't expect to spend much time in the Casa Grande area, but it's nice to know we've got a couple of places to park if we need to.

Monday, October 18, we returned to California for our appointment at Acacia RV. Driving through Quartzite, Arizona on Interstate 10, we saw several RVs dry camping on BLM land just outside town, but nowhere near the numbers that will swell the population of this tiny desert outpost in January and February. Every winter thousands of RVers make their annual pilgrimage to Quartzite to boondock in the sun far away from the cold weather up north. We've never experienced Quartzite, but every serious RVer needs to, at least once.

Quartzite reminds us of an old west boom town - one of those hastily thrown together communities that sprang up wherever gold, silver or some other precious commodity was discovered. As the miners poured in, saloons, stores and other businesses, some respectable and others not so respectable, seemed to grow out of the bare ground overnight in all sorts of makeshift accom-

Meandering Down The Highway

modations. Not that Quartzite's businesses are shady in any way, as far as we know. But as you drive through town, you'll see swap meets and roadside vendors conducting business out of tents, selling everything from sunglasses to solar panels and whatever else the vast numbers of RVers who will soon swarm over the desert may need. It's almost a carnival atmosphere, and everyone should come and see it one time in their lives. Many of the RVers we've met wouldn't think of missing Quartzite during the winter. We plan to be a part of the fun this year.

Interstate 10 as you come into California reminded us of Interstate 40 across northern New Mexico. What *do* some of these states do with all of their highway tax money, anyway? It's obvious they darn sure don't spend it on road repairs. And could someone tell me what California has against mile markers? Every other highway I've ever driven in the nation has those neat little green mileposts along the sides of the road, and the exits are numbered to correspond with the mile markers. But not in California. You just sort of guess where you are and hope you're at least close.

We spent Monday night at Indian Waters RV Resort in Indio, and would have liked to spend more time in the area, but we needed to get to Acacia RV for our repair work. I've driven through the Indio area several times, but never stopped except for gas. The slower RV lifestyle allows us to stop for a while and really get to know an area. We made plans to spend a few days in Indio once our appointment in Colton was behind us.

We stopped at the Camping World in San Bernardino, California to drop off a few newspapers and got a real scare. As we were turning onto the freeway on-ramp to get back onto the Interstate, a car made a wide turn in front of us, crossing into our lane as he cut in front of us. I swerved hard to avoid a collision, throwing Miss Terry around in her seat and rattling a few things inside the rig, but we were okay. I can't believe how rude and

Meandering Down The Highway

reckless some drivers are.

Fleetwood Flops

At noon Tuesday, October 19, we arrived at Acacia RV, hoping that if we got there a bit early they would have the extra time to assess our problems and maybe get a head start on the repairs. We knew right off something was wrong when the "full Fleetwood repair facility" the factory representative had told us about was a small old building surrounded by a chain link fence. The young lady inside the office had no idea who we were or why we were there. It turned out that since our appointment had been made through Fleetwood three weeks earlier, the company had undergone major changes. Steve, the partner I had spoken with, was no longer with the company, they had just moved to their present location a matter of days earlier and everything was in a state of confusion. We were directed to park on the side of the building until the owner arrived.

Five hours of baking in the hot sun later, the owner arrived to tell us he had absolutely no knowledge of our appointment. He read our list of repairs needed and promised to call Fleetwood the first thing next morning. When the appointment was made the first time around, we were told the repair facility had hookups where we could park while the work was begin completed. As it turned out, we were allowed to plug into electricity overnight, and instructed not to try to leave the area, since the gate would be locked and an alarm would sound if we got too near the fence. Since it didn't look like too great a neighborhood, we weren't planning on going anywhere.

The next morning, after a lot of head scratching and mumbling, the folks at Acacia RV told us that they were no longer a Fleetwood repair facility, but that Fleetwood had made arrangements for us to go to Mike Thompson's, nearby. Meanwhile the ram had completely failed on our bedroom slide, dumping the hydraulic fluid into the compartment under the bed.

Meandering Down The Highway

We refilled the fluid reservoir, got the slide back in and drove to Mike Thompson's.

Nick Payne, the service writer, and Kent Fink, the mechanic at Thompson's tried to accommodate us. Out of 17 repairs needed, Fleetwood would only authorize seven. As it turned out, the ram needed for the slide was not available at the factory, nor was the gasket needed for our oven door. We were told it could take anywhere from one to six weeks to get the parts. The gaps around the slide out seals, which allowed bugs into the rig at night, were "repaired" by gluing bits of weather stripping around them. This repair lasted until the first time we ran out the slides, when the patches fell off. After several hours over two days in Mike Thompson's repair facility, all that was accomplished was adjusting the driver and main doors and replacement of a reading lamp and the weatherstripping on the screen door. We spent the night parked on the street in front of the repair shop, and you can bet we weren't happy campers.

Friday morning I called Al, our contact at Fleetwood, again and told him our opinion of Fleetwood's products and services. To drive over 250 miles and not have the parts necessary to complete the repairs, and be told we would have to return again in several weeks was just not acceptable. Al said he'd call back the same day, but of course, what Fleetwood *says* they will do and what they actually *do* are not always the same thing. We never heard a word. Monday morning, after three tries, I finally connected with Al at Fleetwood, had to explain the problem all over again from day one, and received yet another promise that the company would take care of the problem. The latest news from Fleetwood is that they'll order the parts needed and send them to a shop in Arizona to complete the work. Wait a minute, weren't we just in Arizona? Didn't we leave Arizona to come back to California for repairs? Stop the merry-go-round, I want to get off! I've met a lot of people who love their Pace Arrows,

Meandering Down The Highway

Bounders, Southwinds and other Fleetwood RVs. But in my opinion folks, based on our experience, if anyone ever tries to sell you a Fleetwood product, run, do not walk, for the nearest exit.

We were beginning to think that we were alone in our troubles with Fleetwood, until someone sent me the web address for another Fleetwood customer who has had an even worse experience. If you have Internet access, check it out at www.geocities.com/Baja/Trails/5935

(An Update on the Fleetwood situation: After having us drive from Arizona to California to get the repairs needed, and bouncing us from one repair shop to another in California over a period of several days, Fleetwood made arrangements to have the parts needed sent to Biddulph RV in Glendale, Arizona and coordinated an appointment with Biddulph's service department. The morning of our appointment, I called Biddulph to be sure everything was ready, only to learn that Fleetwood had dropped the ball yet again! No parts had been shipped, and the appointment was rescheduled. In the meantime, the RV has developed a crack in the fiberglass on the side, extending for several inches from where the slide out room comes out.)

RV Shopping

While we were in Colton waiting for repairs, we visited Altman's Winnebago, just across the street from Mike Thompson's. Sales representative Chris Hannon introduced us to the Mountain Aire RV line, made by Newmar. Now folks, this diesel pusher is a great rig. Unfortunately we're a bit upside down in our Pace Arrow, and given all of the problems with it, no dealer we've spoken to has been too eager to take it in trade. Even though he knew we weren't ready to purchase yet, Chris spent a lot of time talking to us, took us on a test drive and really showed us what a good RV dealership means by customer service. Not at all like Earnhardt's, where we purchased our rig. The salesman we purchased our Pace Arrow from couldn't wait to get out of our

Meandering Down The Highway

sight as soon as the papers were signed. Given all that has happened with the rig, from misrepresenting the size of the engine to the poor quality of the rig, we understand now that he had reason to make himself scarce. We'd really like to learn more about the Mountain Aire diesel pushers. If any of our readers drive one, or have owned one, I'd really appreciate your comments, good or bad.

We spent a day at the big RV show in Pomona, and went into RV overload. There were hundreds of rigs to choose from, everything from high line diesel coaches to tiny pop-up campers. The vendors' tent had displays of products ranging from tow bars to satellite antennae, and everything in between. We ran into our new friends Ed and Gloria Helmuth at the Escapees booth, and were able to meet Joe and Kay Peterson, founders of the Escapees Club. Kay is a darling lady, absolutely delightful, and the seminar on RVing she and Joe put on was excellent. If you're new to RVing or are thinking about purchasing an RV, you really need to attend one of the big RV shows held around the country. You'll find hundreds of RVs of every size and description to choose from.

Folks, I'll tell you, some of those top dollar RVs are amazing. We walked into one that was listed at $775,000. I was afraid to ask if at that price they'd throw in a tank of fuel with the purchase. Seems to me they should throw in an entire Mideast country when you're spending that kind of money. We walked into one big rig that had so much red velvet, mirrored ceilings and walls that I thought I was in a house of ill repute. (Not that I've ever *been* in a house of ill repute, mind you, but I had a friend who was in one once, and he told me all about it.) But I got to thinking, if a fellow *really* wanted to make some money on the road... never mind.

Desert Nomads

We drove up to Victorville Friday afternoon for the gun

Meandering Down The Highway

show, which was a total waste of time. No one was buying, and we left the show early Saturday, deciding not to even waste our time Sunday. We visited the Roy Rogers - Dale Evans Museum in Victorville and spent several hours transported back in time to the days when cowboys rode the silver screen.

From Victorville, we drove east on State Highway 18 through Apple Valley, Lucerne Valley, then turned onto Highway 247 to connect with Interstate 10 to Western Horizon's Desert Pools Resort at Desert Hot Springs. The resort features three hot tubs fed by mineral hot springs, and soaking in them was wonderful. Several kinks soaked themselves away and we were totally relaxed when we got back to our rig.

Just west of Lucerne Valley on Highway 18, we spotted two historical markers and stopped to investigate. The markers record information on a battle between Indians and Whites in southern California, at Chimney Rock, on February 16, 1867. The incident happened after Indians raided and burned cabins and a sawmill in the San Bernardino Mountains. A posse was formed and attacked the Indians at their village, killing many and driving the survivors into the desert. It was the last skirmish with Indians in southern California. Anglo encroachment into the Indians' traditional homelands eventually consumed the territory.

Coming into Lucerne Valley, we spotted a sign for Teddy Bear's Salvage and Antiques. We were reminded of the old *Sanford and Son* television program by all of the trash and treasures strewn through the yard of the place. Also in Lucerne Valley, we spotted an iron cage with a huge stuffed moose standing in it sitting alongside the highway. We couldn't find a place to pull off to take a picture, but we had to speculate on what it was doing there. Did someone have a house too small to hold their hunting trophy? Sort of like building a boat in the basement and not having a door it will fit through?

Meandering Down The Highway

Outside of Landers, the road suddenly takes a severe dip, probably 15 percent or better, with no warning. Poor Miss Terry was looking at a road map when we hit it, and looked up just in time to feel like the earth had dropped out from under us. She said it was a good two minutes before she could breathe again. We're not roller coaster people.

There's a very unique type of farm just outside of Palm Springs - a wind farm. Huge windmills cover the foothills of the mountains, generating energy from the wind that is converted to electricity. We toured the wind farm, and were impressed with the technology. With our world's shrinking natural resources, we need to explore every form of alternate energy we can.

I think Mel and Jeanette Gray are stalking me. We first ran into them at Ocean City, Washington, then our paths crossed again at Verde River Resort. We weren't at Desert Pools an hour before we discovered our friends were in the resort too. Spend any time on the road at all and you'll never be lonely. Over and over again you'll run into friends you met somewhere else, often clear across the country. Within just a couple of hours at Desert Pools we ran into three or four other people whom we have met at other RV parks.

RV people are among the friendliest you'll find anywhere. Wander through any RV park and you'll see people of all ages sitting under awnings chatting casually, with no regard to their economic status or who they are back in the "real" world. Our first evening at Desert Pools, an older couple from Canada were out for a stroll. We called out a hello from under our awning, and they stopped to visit. We talked an hour or two, relating our adventures on the road, comparing notes on RV parks we have visited and trips we've made or plan to take. The next evening the resort held a steak fry, and we joined three other couples at a table. Soon we were all talking like we'd been friends forever. There are no

Meandering Down The Highway

strangers in the world of RVing.

RVers are also among the most neighborly folks you'll ever find. I was having a problem with my television antenna while we were staying at Verde River Resort and asked a neighbor for advice. He couldn't figure it out either, but he went off in search of someone who could, and was back soon with another RVer who solved the problem in a matter of minutes. Recently while we were staying at Desert Pools in California, we went off exploring for the afternoon and a stiff wind came up. The air was calm when we left and we had left our awning down. Driving back to the RV park, I mentioned to Miss Terry that I was afraid our awning may have been damaged in the wind. We needn't have worried, when we got back to our rig, someone had lowered the awning in our absence. We have no idea who the Good Samaritan was, just another friendly RVer looking out for his neighbor.

Many RVers we've met work or have part time businesses to supplement their incomes. Some are too young to retire and work full time. We have a couple of gigs going - the *Gypsy Journal*, of course, which is our main activity, as well as selling accessories at gun shows, and repairing windshields on RVs. If you want to travel, full or part time, you can make it happen. We're proof of that, as are many other RVers we've met.

It was still hot in the desert during the daytime while we were in California, and we ran the air conditioner most days. But when the sun set, it was very pleasant to sit outside under the stars.

We're adding a few paid advertisements to the *Gypsy Journal* with this issue. Don't worry, there'll always be plenty of new adventures to share with you and we won't sacrifice the space needed to tell you about the RV lifestyle for the sake of advertising. But the added income from advertising helps us make ends meet and insures that we can continue to travel and write about what we see and do. We appreciate you patronizing our advertisers, and when you do, please tell them you heard

Meandering Down The Highway

about them in the *Gypsy Journal*.

Thursday, October 28 we headed back to Arizona to await the arrival of the parts needed for our repairs. At Chiriaco Summit, California we stopped at the General Patton Museum, located in the Mohave Desert where Patton trained his army for combat in North Africa during World War II. The museum is a must-see for any history buff, with displays of tanks, weapons, military equipment and information on the war years and the people who served during that terrible time.

One thing that really caught our attention in the museum is a huge three dimensional map of the Mohave Desert that was constructed as part of the Colorado River Aqueduct program. I've lived in the Southwest for many years and traveled extensively throughout the area, but I never got a real picture of just how vast and rugged the region is until viewing the map. I think you'll find it impressive.

The California Department of Corrections had a work crew at the museum doing some landscaping. Several orange-shirted inmates were wielding axes, shovels, and picks against the baked desert ground, improving the trails at the museum. Some people may be just a bit disconcerted at the sight of convicts using such potentially dangerous weapons, but we were comforted by the sight of their guard, stretched out in the back seat of the prison van taking a nap while his charges worked. That's right, the guard was taking a siesta while five or six prison inmates were wandering around unattended! Our tax dollars at work. Sleep well tonight. Actually, I'm sure they were minimum security inmates (at least I hope so) and we had to pass through them to get into the museum's outside display area. Miss Terry was wearing shorts, and I think she was a bit tentative at first, but she had nothing to worry about, they were perfect gentlemen. Well, except for this one guy named Sweaty Eddie, who pinched me on the butt.... but

Meandering Down The Highway

I don't want to talk about it!

I've discovered a neat website for all of you computer using RVers out there. It's www.tellalltravel.com and allows users to list their experiences, both good and bad, with campgrounds, hotels, and such. It's interesting to see what the customers have to say about some of the places out there. Anyone who has been RVing very long knows that the ratings in campground directories are more closely tied to the size of an advertisement purchased than with how good a campground really is. This website could come in handy to steer you toward (or away from) a particular RV park on your next trip.

Well, that's about it for another issue. I'm afraid that due to the unexpected delays for repairs, we're behind schedule and this issue is going out a few days late. We'll do our best to do better next time, and we appreciate your patience. We've covered a lot of ground, and we're having more fun than is probably legal without some sort of permit or license. In the next few weeks we plan on wandering over toward New Mexico and Texas, and maybe along the Gulf Coast if time permits. We never know exactly where we'll be at any given time - we just sort of head in a general direction and then let the wind and our whims steer us to new adventures and places to see. It's more fun that way. But wherever we travel, there are always new friends to meet, and new places to discover around every corner. We'll tell you all about them next issue. Until then, hope to see you in our travels.

Meandering Down The Highway

Meandering Down The Highway

January-February, 2000

After being broken down for over a month, we at last had some good news. Someone at Fleetwood finally put aside their crossword puzzle, drained their coffee cup, and located a ram for our bedroom slide-out, and it was installed November 23. The next day we made it back onto the road at last, and it was a wonderful feeling to see that white line on the highway rolling out in front of us.

The only good thing to come out of our unscheduled down time was that we were in Mesa, Arizona, where Miss Terry's folks are spending the winter. My son Travis lives just a few miles away in Scottsdale, so we had plenty of time to spend with the family. But if we ever had even a hint of suspicion about whether our hearts are out on the open road, it was erased as the weeks slowly dragged on. In one of her books on fulltiming, Kay Peterson, who founded the Escapees Club with her husband Joe, refers to a malady called hitch fever - the need to get on down the road. We sure had a bad case, and only after we hit the highway did we feel any relief.

One thing about the big city - look around long enough and you'll see just about anything. One afternoon Miss Terry and I were traveling along the Superstition Freeway in the Phoenix area when Terry noticed that the fellow driving the car next to us was reading a book. Now, I'm not talking about glancing quickly at something while traffic is at a standstill. This fool was driving

Meandering Down The Highway

down the highway during rush hour with a paperback novel propped up on the steering wheel, reading! We were stuck next to him for two or three miles, and never saw him lift his eyes from the page. Hey fellow, put the book down! You're in a car, not a *bathroom*!

When we dropped our RV off for the repair work, we met Tom and Nancy Vineski, fellow Escapees and fulltimers. It's always a delight to meet new RVing friends, and Tom and Nancy were no exception. They've been on the road quite a few years now, and operate a business called Alternatives, specializing in RV solar systems and other energy efficient products that help folks sever the umbilical cord connecting them to the electric power grid. We've been wanting to learn more about solar energy and its benefits for RVers, and Tom and Nancy are a wealth of information. There's a lot of hype out there, and just like some used car salesmen (and RV salesmen too), you'll have no problem finding plenty of people who will tell you their product is the only system you need. Tom and Nancy cut right to the chase and told us what we did, and didn't need, for our lifestyle. They're friends we know we'll enjoy spending more time with as we meet up somewhere down the road.

In our last issue, I mentioned a neat modem setup that allows a laptop computer to be connected to a digital or cellular telephone, so RVers can send and receive e-mail without the benefit of a regular telephone connection. My in-laws, Pete and Bess Weber, made us an early Christmas present of the modem, and we find it works just fine. Not as fast as a land line, maybe, but still pretty darn good. We use America Online, and even with all of the graphics they put out, I was able to send nine e-mail letters I had written offline, as well as downloading four new messages, all in less than four minutes after connecting. Connecting can take a little extra time, but at other times I get on with the first attempt. Just for the sake of experimentation, I also opened the e-bay

...ering Down The Highway

...rday evening, and though it took almost a
...ce in I could access our account. The cost
... cruising the Internet with this setup a bit
... e-mail tasks, I'm impressed. Isn't

... .m. November 24 and headed south on
... ush hour traffic. We reached Tucson
... on the interstate in Tucson is nothing
... in Phoenix. The interstate crosses
... on on the west side, and most of the
... west on surface streets. But after
we ... heavy on the highway all the way
to E... day before Thanksgiving, we expected that
there ...ght be a lot of travelers on the road.

Benson has had a major growth spurt with the development of Kartchner Caverns, the new state park that has grown up around the magnificent cave which opened as a state park earlier in November. Benson has new lodging facilities, gas stations, restaurants and all of the other services needed to support the visitor traffic that is expected to flow into the area to see the cave. When you consider that the San Pedro Valley and Cochise County also have attractions including the Old West town of Tombstone, Fort Huachuca, Bisbee, Cochise Stronghold, and pleasant weather pretty much year 'round, you can understand why it has been popular with tourists, RVers and snowbirds for a long time. The new state park just adds to the choices of places to visit.

We arrived at Western Horizons Twin Lakes Resort in St. David, a few miles south of Benson, at about 6 p.m. This time of year, it's dark by then, but we had called ahead and asked the nice folks in the office to hold a site for us. After stopping at the dump station, we backed into our space, hooked up water, electric and

Meandering Down The Highway

TV cable and flipped on a couple of electric space heaters to beat back the chilly night air.

Thanksgiving morning we woke up to find that our water hose had frozen overnight. Fortunately, we always keep about a quarter tank of fresh water in our holding tank, so we were in fine shape until the sun warmed things up and thawed the hose. We drove down to Tombstone and wandered the old board sidewalks for a while. I've always loved Tombstone for all of the history the frontier town holds, and even on a holiday quite a few of the stores and shops were open. Unfortunately, over time, commercialism has taken hold, as it inevitably must. Today people stand on the sidewalks hawking gunfight re-enactments in the places where such western legends as Doc Holliday, the Clantons, and the Earp brothers once shot their way into history. I mean, Johnny Ringo's Saloon was even pushing cappuccino! I think old Wyatt must be turning over in his grave.

We stopped by the Escapees Saguaro Co-op in Benson to drop off a stack of newspapers, and they were setting up the club house to serve Thanksgiving dinner. When the folks there learned we were Escapees, they wouldn't listen to any excuses - we *were* going to stay for the Thanksgiving meal, no arguments accepted. Miss Terry and I both get a bit shy at times, but that just doesn't work around Escapees, or SKPs, as they call themselves. When you are an Escapee, you become a member of an extended family of RVers around the country, and SKPs just won't tolerate their family members being alone on a holiday.

The club house was packed with happy, chatting people of all ages, and our table included several nice couples who made us feel so welcome we wondered why we would have ever been hesitant to join in all the fun in the first place. Elliot and Ruth Oren were seated across from us. The Oren's have been fulltiming for almost ten years, and we picked up several good tips from them

Meandering Down The Highway

during our meal. One thing about RVers, be they Escapees or not, everyone you run into is always happy to offer advice and support to their fellow vagabonds.

The Escapees were planning to hold a dance Thanksgiving evening and wanted us to stay, but we needed to get on the road early the next morning, so we reluctantly backed off and returned to our rig at Twin Lakes Resort.

We Visit A Real Ghost Town

Friday morning we headed east on Interstate 10, through the interesting rock formations of Texas Canyon, where Apaches used to ambush stagecoaches and cavalry patrols, and crossed into New Mexico. Just a couple of miles into New Mexico, the old railroad ghost town of Steins sits hard by the interstate. I've always wanted to visit Steins, and this seemed like as good a time as any. What a treat! Unlike so many Old West ghost towns, which have been commercialized, Steins is a real ghost town. You won't find any costumed gunfighters or shady ladies here, no shops peddling tomahawks made in Taiwan, and there wasn't a drop of cappuccino to be found. Just two really neat people, and the remains of a town that once thrived and now has been passed on by time. My kind of place.

Larry and Linda Link, owners of Steins, have purposely kept the place original as they've slowly brought the former railroad stop back to life, and it's a true labor of love. I knew I had found a kindred soul in Larry, a bearded man with shaggy hair and a great sense of humor. Within five minutes of shaking hands, we had set women's liberation, Bambi lovers and tree huggers, and most of the rest of the politically correct modern world back about twenty years. When I mentioned how afraid I am of snakes, Larry agreed. About that time someone piped up and said "Those snakes are as afraid of you as you are of them!" My new buddy Larry was fast on the return, claiming "No they're not! If they

Meandering Down The Highway

were, they'd carry a gun like I do!" You can't spend much time in Larry's presence without doing a lot of chuckling.

Linda told us she and Larry have known each other since they were five years old, and have been dating since they were fifteen. Linda is obviously a very patient woman. After all, she left the bright lights of Phoenix to move to the middle of the desert with her man. I guess maybe she figured the further away from civilization she could keep Larry, the better it was for all concerned. Look for a feature story on Steins in this issue, and the next time you're in southern New Mexico, stop in and check the place out.

Just west of Deming, New Mexico, a billboard touts the town as a place of "pure water and fast ducks." I assume the latter refers to Deming's famed Great American Duck Races, held every August (unless it has something to do with lonely farmers out in the middle of the desert, in which case, I don't want to talk about it). We pulled into the Escapees Dream Catcher RV Park in Deming about 3 p.m., and received the same warm welcome from managers Glen and Betty Corum that we have in every Escapee park we've visited. At the regular 4 p.m. friendship hour, a bunch of SKPs gathered in the club house to swap stories, talk about the places they've been, and the places they're going. This fellowship of travelers we're a part of makes it impossible to be lonely when you're on the road and far from family and familiar faces.

Into The Lone Star State

Saturday morning we continued on to Texas, stopping for fuel at the Flying J in Anthony, just outside El Paso. I computed the mileage and we were up to 6.18 miles per gallon, a nice increase over what we have been getting. Every RVer should join Flying J's Real Value Club. There is no cost to join, and you'll receive a map showing all Flying J locations across the country, as well as an RV Club Card that you insert into a card reader before pumping your fuel. You'll receive a one cent discount per

Meandering Down The Highway

gallon on gasoline or diesel purchases, five cents per gallon on propane, and can earn additional discounts based on non-fuel purchases. Flying J's have free RV dump stations, special fuel islands reserved for RVs, free Internet hookups in their restaurants, and they even let you park overnight for free, if you can sleep through all the truck noise. We've found that across the country, their fuel prices are competitive with other local fuel suppliers, before you factor in the RV Club discount. We make it a point to patronize RV friendly businesses such as Flying J, Wal-Mart, and Cracker Barrel General Stores. It's that old you scratch my back and I'll scratch yours thing at work.

The Texas Welcome Center in El Paso had a huge supply of brochures for just about every community in the state, and we loaded up. You'd be surprised at the number of neat little out of the way places you'll discover when you make it a habit of browsing through the racks of literature in state welcome centers. We make them our first stop when we come into a new state.

Driving through El Paso, I found myself humming the old Marty Robbins tune by the same name. It's been at least 15 years since I've been to El Paso, the city has grown, but traffic on Interstate 10 wasn't bad. We rolled through without incident and began the long, boring drive across the state that's so big it dwarfs most European countries.

I know why they call it Texas, since the place is so big that it seems like it "takes us" forever to get through it. Actually, there's so much to see and do in Texas that it would take years to see it all. From miles of beaches to mountains to deserts and fresh water lakes full of fighting bass, not to mention more history that you can ever see, Texas has something to offer everyone.

We stopped at Comanche Land RV Park in Fort Stockton for the night, a small park that is a great bargain at $10 a night. While Miss Terry whipped up a batch of her delicious chicken fajitas, I stretched out on the sofa and let a few of the highway kinks

Meandering Down The Highway

unwind. That lady I married is one fine cook, and even though our new mobile lifestyle has forced her into a kitchen that's one-tenth the size of her former domain, it hasn't hampered her style or output at all.

Before we left Fort Stockton the next morning, we drove into town to see Piasano Pete, the town's resident roadrunner. They say everything's bigger in Texas, and old Pete's no exception. The roadrunner statue measures eleven feet high and 22 feet long.

We've all heard of the Road Kill Cafe. Well, I've decided they stock their kitchen from the highways of west Texas. We seemed to average at least one dead deer for every mile, their carcasses piled up along the roadway mile after gory mile. November is hunting season, and it seems the weapon of choice in the Lone Star state must be the three-quarter ton Ford pickup, with the optional four wheel drive, roll bar, and brush guard. We also spotted a few live animals, including deer, hawks, and an armadillo that Terry saw waddling alongside the highway.

At Ozona, we detoured off the highway to visit the small downtown park and it's David Crockett Memorial. Crockett, legendary frontiersman and one of the heros of the Alamo, is revered in Texas. The little park in Ozona was well worth the stop. Early on a Sunday morning, few people were out and about and we had the place to ourselves. We walked past the gazebo under the park's big old trees, fallen leaves crunching under our feet, and paused to look at the memorial, as well as several other small plaques and a statue dedicated to early day pioneers.

If you need gasoline, don't stop in Segovia. We passed by Junction, where signs said gas was going for $1.25, figuring we might save a couple of pennies a gallon down the road. Forty miles later, in Segovia, it was $1.35 and $1.40, depending on which bandit you wanted to give your money to. There are plenty of places like this out in the middle of nowhere who are not at all hesitant to stick it to you, taking advantage of travelers they figure

Meandering Down The Highway

they'll never see again anyway. With those kind of prices, you can bet they won't see us again. But our fuel gauge was sitting on empty, so we bit the bullet and filled up. We were not happy campers when we exited the highway in Kerrville and fuel was going for $1.19 a gallon. The only good news was that our mileage was up even more, to 7.07 mpg. I recently poured a couple of bottles of STP fuel system cleaner into the gas tank. I don't know if that had anything to do with our improved economy, but considering the low of 5.04 mpg we were getting a couple of months ago, we're not complaining. One RVer we spoke to suggested that since our odometer just reached 16,000 miles, maybe the engine's getting broken in and mileage will be better.

You know it's November when you drive through a small town and see banners hanging over the main street welcoming hunters. Several of the small towns we passed through were going out of their way to make hunters (and their money) feel welcome. We left the Interstate at Kerrville and turned south on Highway 173 through rolling hill country and past several beautiful mansions. Bandera is an interesting little town, with quite a few antique shops and restaurants we wanted to check out, but it was getting late in the day and we needed to get to the Escapees park in Hondo before the office closed. We made a mental note to return to Bandera in the future.

Highway 90 through Hondo was lined with miniature billboards that local businesses and organizations had erected as holiday greetings, giving the town a very homey feeling. The Escapees Lone Star Co-op is about seven miles west of Hondo. The folks at the park made us feel right at home, and we settled in for a couple of days visit.

The Shrine Of Texas Liberty

As a dedicated history nut, I've wanted to visit the Alamo for as long as I can remember. I used to jokingly say I would probably

Meandering Down The Highway

never make it, since you have to drive through Texas forever just to get there. After our visit to the old mission where 189 Texas patriots sacrificed themselves in the struggle for independence, I realized it would have been worth *walking* through Texas to experience.

The Alamo is located in downtown San Antonio, dwarfed by modern skyscrapers, but the moment you step onto the grounds you can feel the ghosts of those brave men who struggled here all around you. We've included a feature on the Alamo in this issue, and to me, it was one of the highlights of our travels thus far.

After our visit to the Alamo, we strolled along San Antonio's famous River Walk, where sidewalk cafes offer the opportunity to enjoy anything from a bucket of crabs to fine French dining while they watch the river and the pedestrian traffic flow by.

We were pleasantly surprised at how easy the highways were to navigate in San Antonio. Traffic was light both going in and on the return trip, making for a pleasant drive. Here's a hint when you visit downtown San Antonio - leave your RV in the park where you're staying and drive your tow vehicle. Even if you could find a place to park, who wants to drive a huge rig through downtown traffic? If you park at the River Center Mall, just a block or two from the Alamo, the stores will validate your parking ticket, giving you two hours free. There's a lot to see and do in San Antonio, and you could easily spend a week and not be able to take it all in.

Texas Nomads

We stayed at Hondo for two days before heading east, rolling through small towns, farming country, and past uncounted antique shops and restaurants selling barbecue, chili, and catfish. You can tell which part of the country you're in by the fare restaurants specialize in. When we were on the coast, seafood was everywhere. In Arizona and New Mexico, steak is the food of choice. In Texas it's chili and barbecue, and as we travel

Meandering Down The Highway

eastward, more and more we see signs advertising catfish. My stomach loves traveling as much as my brain.

Just west of Navasota, on Highway 105, we pulled off into a picnic area where a plaque said that this area of Lee County (named for Confederate general Robert E. Lee) was home to a group of northern European people called the Wend. Lee County and a small area in Australia are the only places where Wendese, the native language of the Wend people, is spoken. Much of central and west Texas was settled by European immigrants, especially Germans, and their heritage is evident in many of the bakeries and other businesses that specialize in German food and pastries.

We were pleasantly surprised to discover that most of the highways we traveled on in Texas were very good. Off the interstates, U.S. highways, and even many of the State highways are four lane divided roads, making traveling easy and comfortable. There are frequent rest areas and picnic areas on every highway where you can pull off the road for a break or a pit stop. The majority of them are handicapped accessible. Texas seems to be RV and tourist friendly, unlike some states we've visited or heard of. In fact, quite a few Texas towns allow free overnight parking for RVers in their public parks, and many even have electric and water hookups, along with dump stations. It's this attitude, along with their very reasonable rates for registering RVs that has helped many fulltimers choose Texas as their legal domicile.

We've stayed in several Western Horizons RV resorts, but we both think we've discovered the best yet - Lake Conroe Marina and RV Resort, just north of the city of Conroe, Texas. Our parking site was right on the shore of the lake, the back of the rig about ten feet from the water's edge. Fishermen pull some fine bass and catfish from Lake Conroe, and the minute I saw the beautiful lake, my fingers were itching to wrap around a fishing

Meandering Down The Highway

rod.

We originally planned to visit Lake Conroe for only a day or two, but one look at our setting and I went up to the office to reserve our spot for two weeks. That's one of the great things about the fulltime lifestyle, when you reach a place you want to spend some time in, you have that latitude. There's usually no pressing schedule pushing you on down the road before you're ready to go. The resort was fairly empty, it being the off season, but the neighbors we had were all friendly and made us feel welcome. Even the flocks of ducks and geese who inhabit the lake are friendly. As we sat outside at our picnic table on our first morning at the resort, two geese consummated their courtship under our RV.

Using Lake Conroe as a base, we did a bit of exploring, checking out the small towns nearby. When we spotted the tiny post office in Cut and Shoot, Texas, I just had to stop. Being the wise guy I am, I wanted to ask the postmaster if the Cut and Shoot post office is where they send disgruntled postal workers for basic training. (My buddy Billy Bob Butler, Lakeside, Arizona's resident postmaster and mad balloonist, hates it when I make disgruntled postal worker jokes.) But as it turned out, I never got an answer to my question - the Cut and Shoot post office was closed. A sign on the door said the post office is open daily from 8:30 a.m until 2:18 p.m. why 2:18 p.m.? Isn't that an odd time? Why 2:18? Why not 2:12, or 3:16, or even 1:07? I'd love to find out, but I'm kind of afraid of pushing those postal people too far.

Speaking of post offices, we'll file this one under "Boy, do I feel dumb." I ran into the post office in Conroe one day to mail a few items, and got a bit lost. Stopping in a gas station for directions (Yes, this man isn't ashamed to ask for directions. If I had been, we'd never have gotten out of our home town), I was told to go down the street three lights and turn left. Approaching the intersection I needed, I pulled into the left turn lane, directly

Meandering Down The Highway

behind a large semi-truck. A moment later another vehicle pulled in behind me, then a third, and we all waited for the traffic to move. I couldn't see around the big truck, but waited as traffic in the through lanes moved on, new cars stopped next to me, then moved on again. I realized it was taking a long time for us to move forward, but since all I could see was the back of the semi, I just sat patiently. After several minutes, the woman in the car behind me got out and came up to my window. "So, do you feel dumb yet?" she asked me. My mama taught me never to lie to ladies, so I replied "I feel dumb most of the time. Why?" She jerked her thumb over her shoulder toward the semi. "Because no one's in that truck. It's parked about a hundred feet from the corner, right here in the center lane." I have no idea why the truck was sitting there unattended, but apparently when I pulled up behind it, the rest of the traffic just followed me. They then patiently followed me as I pulled around the truck and finally up to the traffic signal. Gosh, it sure felt uncomfortable with all those eyes staring at the back of my head until the light changed and I could drive away!

We haven't experienced much rain since we've been on the road, but December 2nd we made up for that. The skies opened up and it poured. It was raining so hard the rats and lawyers were coming up from the sewers. Strong winds and heavy rain continued for three days, keeping us inside much of the time. Occasionally there would be a break in the clouds and the sun would peek out, but it didn't last longer than a few minutes, and then the rain would pound down again. A couple of times the wind gusts were so strong I halfway expected the RV to take flight.

Making New Friends

It would be pretty hard to travel fulltime in an RV and not make new friends. Everywhere we go, our fellow RVers, be they fulltimers, extended travelers, or those who use their RVs only for recreational use have proven to be a friendly group who are

Meandering Down The Highway

always happy to stop and pass the time of day or invite us over to the recreation hall or club house for an ice cream social or some other get together. We've met people from all walks of life in our travels, and all have been simply wonderful, sharing travel tips and encouraging our efforts with the *Gypsy Journal*.

The folks we meet are always happy to share their hobbies and interests as well. We've had people introduce us to interesting things like ham radio, rock hounding, off road four wheeling, fly fishing, and their favorite crochet patterns. There's not much you could want to learn about that someone in an RV park doesn't have some experience with.

The stereotypical RVers are senior citizens, spending their golden years traveling around the country visiting the grandkids and playing shuffleboard. While the majority of RVers may well be retired, more and more baby boomers are taking to the road, many traveling fulltime and working as they go. Not to mention the younger RVers we've met who home school their children as they show them the world. RVing isn't just for couples, either. We've also run into quite a few single people, both men and women, enjoying life on the road.

One real treat for us is to meet up with the people who subscribe to the *Gypsy Journal* as we travel. Among our first subscribers were Dick and Elaine Marshall, from Lawrenceville, Georgia, who were at Lake Conroe Resort and stopped by to visit. More and more people are subscribing every week, and meeting them in person helps put a face with the name.

Tom and Wynell Hill, from Midwest City, Oklahoma, were also at Lake Conroe, making a shakedown trip in their brand new Dutch Star diesel rig. We sat together at the Saturday evening steak dinner, and struck up a quick friendship as they shared tales of their adventures traveling from border to border and beyond. Other new friends were Louis and Sally St. Marie, fulltimers from Minnesota, along with Glenn and Jayne Bailey, from Towanda,

Meandering Down The Highway

Kansas. We love and dearly miss the good friends we left behind in our home town when we began traveling, but the new friends we make on the road help to fill the vacuum.

Other friends we made at Lake Conroe were quite a few of the ducks and geese who live on the lake. One big white goose, whom I nicknamed Sylvester, came to the rig's door seeking a handout, and when I began feeding it some bread, our relationship was affirmed. Though my feathered friend seemed docile enough, I've learned enough about wild critters over the years that I wouldn't let it eat out of my hand, preferring to throw its bread on the ground. Miss Terry urged me to feed it by hand, but I told her no way, I've been bit by a duck before. "That's not a duck, it's a goose," my pretty lady informed me. "Yeah, well, I've been goosed before too. Forget it, I'm throwing the bread on the ground!"

What with a cold snap that had us running our furnace more than usual, and other routine things like cooking and heating water for the shower and dishes, we found ourselves running pretty low on propane. Since no local company comes into the resort, we drove over to a propane company in nearby Willis to fill up. Coleta, the lovely lady who filled our tank told us that someday she and her husband hope to become fulltime RVers, so we chatted a bit about life on the road. While she was filling our propane tank, we got to talking about the precautions one must follow when working with gas. Our new friend said that working with a flammable fuel such as LP gas is completely safe, as long as one uses common sense. "But did you ever notice how rare common sense is?" she asked. Yes indeed, it does seem to be a pretty scarce commodity from time to time.

We were out dropping off sample copies of the *Gypsy Journal* at RV parks around the Houston area and stopped at Woodland Lakes RV Resort in Conroe. Owner Diane Sanker is

Meandering Down The Highway

just about as friendly as anyone you could ever hope to find. She told me she and her husband Paul were "two crazy people who came out of retirement to spend our kids' inheritance and build this place." Well, they've done a great job, and we plan to spend a couple of days at Woodland Lakes the next time we come through the area. Diane and Paul have paid attention to every detail, and the result is a wonderful park, not very big, but every site has room for any size RV, with full hookups, including cable TV. There is a great, super clean laundry room with dedicated telephone hookup for your modem, and the park features two fishing ponds full of fighting bass and catfish.

Before building the RV park, the couple took a 10,000 mile trip across the country, visiting other parks, picking their owners' brains, deciding what would work and what wouldn't in their new business. The result is something any owner could be proud of, and any RVer will appreciate. We've been in a lot of parks in our travels, and over time many of them begin to run together in your head. But some of them really stand out as places where you feel at home. Woodland Lakes RV Resort is one of them. We spent quite a bit of time visiting Paul and Diane, and I can personally assure you that they are dedicated to their guests.

The nice folks at Camperland Trailer Sales in Conroe also made us welcome and were happy to pass out the newspaper to their customers. We get so much support from the businesses we visit that it makes our job easy.

South Of Houston

One of the day trips we made was south of Houston to the San Jacinto battlefield, and then on to Galveston. Following the massacre at the Alamo, and other atrocities against Texas patriots, Sam Houston's Army of Texas caught up with the Mexican army led by General Santa Anna at San Jacinto, and in less than 18 minutes the battle was over and Texans had won their independence from Mexico. A towering monument was erected

Meandering Down The Highway

on the battleground, and today the San Jacinto Monument is almost as sacred to Texans as the Alamo.

The monument is currently undergoing renovation, and scaffolding hung over the lower section when we visited, but the museum and theater were open. Since we're now transplanted Texans, I can't deny a certain feeling of pride at the museum's impressive displays of the struggle for independence.

Also at the battlefield is the battleship *Texas*, built before World War I and just as impressive today as she must have been the day she was commissioned. Today the *Texas* is a State Historical Park and visitors walk the decks where sailors' feet pounded as they rushed to battle stations in two world wars.

The San Jacinto Battleground is surrounded by a dense industrial area, with refineries and petrochemical plants belching noxious fumes into the air. You'd think that with that much stuff floating in the air, not much could survive breathing it on a daily basis. Not so. The mosquito population around the battleground is more aggressive than any kamikaze that ever aimed his aircraft at the battleship in her glory days. Now, I'm not saying these mosquitos were *big*, but one offered to take my camera and get me an aerial shot of the monument. I said no way, because I'd never met him before and I figured he might just take my Nikon and keep on going with it. My mama didn't raise any fools. I heard that the construction crews restoring the monument were having trouble locating a crane big enough to do the high work, so they've harnessed a half dozen of the local skeeters and put them to work as a flying scaffold. I'm just glad the one that grabbed me dropped me before we got too high off the ground!

Did you ever notice how many songs have been written about Texas cities? Marty Robbins' *El Paso* and *El Paso City*, the *San Antonio Stroll* and *Rose of San Antonio*, the country hit *Fort Worth*, and Glen Campbell's *Galveston*, to name just a few? I

Meandering Down The Highway

don't know if it was the old song that was so popular back when I was in high school that did it, but for whatever reason, Galveston is one of those places I've always wanted to visit. After we left San Jacinto, we continued driving south and crossed the causeway to Galveston.

The day was fading fast, but we had time to walk out on a jetty and watch the local surfers riding the waves, and saw enough of the city to know we want to go back. There are a ton of neat old houses, and seafood restaurants everywhere. When I spotted Joe's Crab Shack, I knew where we were going to have dinner. Years ago I had eaten at a couple of Joe's Crab Shacks back on the east coast, and remembered them for their laid back atmosphere and great food. I'm happy to report that nothing has changed. Still the same friendly welcome and banter with our waiter, the funky decor, and the food, oh the food! We stuffed ourselves on shrimp, crab fingers, and other goodies, and I ate so much the springs on our Toyota pickup sagged even more then usual when I climbed behind the wheel. We'll be returning to Galveston again, no doubt about that.

Of Prisons And Escapees

The only thing I knew about Huntsville, Texas was that it was the location of the Texas State Penitentiary. We visited Huntsville, and discovered a wonderful little community, full of historic sites, neat old buildings and friendly people.

Just south of Huntsville on Interstate 45, a giant statue of Texas patriot Sam Houston towers 65 feet over the countryside. We stopped at the Visitor Center to check out the statue and received a warm Texas welcome from the ladies in the office, who piled us up with brochures, maps, and information on the many places of interest in the Huntsville area. We spent some time in Huntsville, and have included a feature on the Texas prison Museum in Huntsville in this issue.

You have to laugh when you stop to consider that about 40

Meandering Down The Highway

miles east of Huntsville, home of the Texas prison system, is Livingston, home of the Escapees RV Club. I wonder how many RVers on their way through the area have raised a local eyebrow or two when they stop in some Huntsville business and identify themselves as Escapees.

If you're an Escapee, one of your goals in life is paying a visit to Rainbow's End, the headquarters of the premier RV club in the world. Here the club's business affairs are managed, and the club's massive mail forwarding operation keeps literally thousands of pieces of mail a week flowing out to club members wherever they may be traveling in the country.

We pulled into Rainbow's End on Monday afternoon, December 13, and the place was packed with Escapees home for the holidays. We got settled into our space, and before I had the water and electric connections finished, a couple of folks stopped by to welcome us to the park.

We spent a week at Rainbow's End, touring the club's national headquarters, visiting with everybody and becoming official Texans. One of the great things about fulltime RVing is that you can choose your legal domicile. Many fulltimers choose Texas because they use the Escapees mail service, and because the state is very RV friendly. The fact that Texas also does not have an income tax is an added benefit. Registering our rig in Arizona cost $1,700, and in Texas the fee was only $170. Quite a savings. The process of registering our vehicles and obtaining Texas drivers licenses was quite simple, taking only a couple of hours to get all of this completed. Since we already had Arizona licenses, all Texas required was an eye test.

At the 4 p.m. social hour at Rainbow's End, we received a warm reception and met several people who have been reading the *Gypsy Journal*. Betty Henry, known as the Flower Lady, no longer travels, but she lives at Rainbow's End and is famous for presenting the ladies who visit social hour with lilies, which her

Meandering Down The Highway

son Scott grows commercially. Betty is just one of the Escapees who have left the road to live fulltime at Rainbow's End.

A day or two after we arrived, Gil and Gayle Montalvo pulled in next to us in their Mountain Aire, and we knew we had met new friends we will look forward to crossing paths with down the road. Gil is a quadriplegic who uses a wheelchair, and Gayle drives the motorhome. I helped her figure out a problem with their sewer hose, and they invited us into their rig for a visit. In the two days they were parked next to us, we felt a real kinship with the friendly, outgoing couple. Gil's injury is the result of an accident thirteen years ago, soon after they had purchased a Bounder and were ready to hit the road to follow his career as a professional singer. While some of us might become bitter at such a tragedy, Gil's strong faith and winning attitude took the change in stride. Now, with their children grown and out of the home, the Montalvos are finally realizing their dream and are new fulltimers.

Barb and Hobie Hobart, from Acworth, New Hampshire, were also at Rainbow's End, and we spent an evening visiting and comparing notes about life on the road. I'm always pleased with how helpful our fellow RVers are. I had no more mentioned that our satellite dish didn't work before Ed Mason, from New York was carting test equipment into our rig and crawling up on the roof to check things out, discovering the LNB for the dish was broken. It seemed like every night we were at Rainbow's End, someone stopped in to visit. I commented to Miss Terry that even though we had lived in our old home town for many years, and our work brought us into contact with lots of people every day, I couldn't remember ever having so many friends coming through our door back home.

Update On The RV From Hell

Last issue I reported on all of the problems we've had with our Pace Arrow Vision, and Fleetwood's failure to provide any

Meandering Down The Highway

decent customer service. Since we were pretty well disgusted with repeated unfulfilled promises to take care of our long list of problems, I sent copies of that issue to the president of Fleetwood's motorhome division, as well as the honcho in charge of Customer Service.

We got a call from someone at Fleetwood, promising yet again that they'll solve our problems. Since our last issue, we've added to the list of problems the fact that when we used the stove, something seemed to get hot and expand in the burner controls. The only way we could then turn off the stove was to go outside and shut off the propane. Once the stove cooled down and the metal contracted, we could shut the burner off. In addition, the igniter on our water heater only worked about twenty percent of the time. When it did fire, there was a loud whoosh that we suspected was excess propane burning off. Fleetwood's latest game plan is to send us back to the factory in California in April for repairs (our latest contact at Fleetwood promised that within a week or ten days, someone from the company would call to confirm the April appointment, but three weeks later no one has ever called), while they try to get some of the more immediate problems handled at dealer outlets. The only problem is that when we called the dealers Fleetwood referred us to, none of them seemed to be able to find the time to schedule us in. After calling several dealers Fleetwood recommended, we finally located one who would make an appointment for us.

We made an appointment for Monday, December 20 at Ancira Motorhomes in Temple, Texas for repairs to the stove and water heater. The four hour trip from Livingston to Temple was a slow paced enjoyable drive, passing through the small communities of Bryan, Caldwell, Milano, Cameron, and Rogers. Ancira has water and electric hookups and a dump station for customers awaiting repairs. Shortly after we arrived Sunday afternoon, the weather turned cold and we were glad for our dual

Meandering Down The Highway

furnaces. We had experienced a few days of intermittent gloomy skies while we were at Livingston, but every so often the sun would pop out for an hour or two and keep things fairly warm. By the time Monday morning arrived, the weather had taken a definite downturn, with rain, cold temperatures, and reports of sleet in the area.

Service advisor Rick Miller at Ancira Motorhomes, along with everyone else we met there, really went out of their way to take care of what problems they could, getting the burner control and stove top replaced, and water heater working right. Our appointment was for 8 a.m., and shortly after lunch the work was completed. After the runaround we had experienced at so many other repair facilities, the professionalism of the staff at Ancira was both welcome and refreshing.

While our rig was in the shop, we checked out a few RVs in the showroom. That's right, showroom. No wandering around out in the cold for Ancira customers, they had four or five big class A rigs right inside the showroom. Sales representative Lee McKinnerney showed us an absolutely gorgeous Allegro Bus with triple slideouts. You read right, three slideouts! Talk about a roomy motorhome. Even though we're not in a position to replace our lemon just now, as much as we'd love to, Lee took the time to give us a complete demonstration, including maneuvering the huge diesel rig outside for a test drive and back inside when we were done. If our bank account could have handled it, we would have taken that Allegro with us when we left. We both appreciated the lack of high pressure and the welcoming atmosphere at Ancira RV and will keep them in mind when we're ready to purchase. If any of our readers out there would like to share their experiences with the Allegro brand of RVs, we'd sure welcome your input.

I'm always on the lookout for interesting bits of local history

Meandering Down The Highway

and lore, and Rick Miller at Ancira had a great story to tell us. Rick lives in a small community west of Temple known as The Grove. His wife's family has lived there for several generations, and back in the 1930s, her great-grandfather and several friends were enjoying a bit of homebrew on the steps of the one store in town, located at a crossroads, when a fast moving car skidded to a stop and the blonde woman passenger asked directions to a nearby town. Feeling the effects of his happy juice and in a jovial mood, great-grandpa, then a young man, pointed the strangers in the opposite direction, and off they went in a great cloud of dust. A bit later the car roared back into the crossroads, slid sideways and sped off on the right road.

    The good old boys were having a chuckle over the small town prank when a local farmer arrived on the scene and told them the car's occupants had stopped to ask him directions before making a u-turn and going back in the right direction. Things weren't quite so funny several months later when a Texas Ranger showed up in town with a prisoner in tow. The felon pointed to great-grandpa, in his distinctive black hat, and said "That's the man whose life I saved. When Bonnie realized he had given her the wrong directions, she was going to shoot him as we drove past. I slid the car around the corner and threw her aim off so she wouldn't shoot." Thus was averted The Grove's first and only drive-by shooting, and thus ended the community's only visit from infamous gangsters Bonnie and Clyde.

    Wonderful Waco

    The weather had really gotten ugly by Monday afternoon, with a steady drizzle and gusty winds, and the temperature never got much above 40 degrees all day. The nice folks at Ancira Motorhomes told us we were welcome to stay hooked up at their facility for a day or two until the storm passed. Not wanting to get on the highway in such nasty weather, we gladly took them up on

Meandering Down The Highway

their kind offer. I have to figure that any company that goes so far out of its way to accommodate someone who isn't even their customer is a company I want to do business with in the future.

Tuesday morning the sky was still grey, but the rain had stopped. About 10 a.m. we headed toward Waco, about 40 miles north of Temple on Interstate 35. Waco is home to Baylor University, the Texas Ranger Museum, the Dr. Pepper Museum, the Texas Sports Hall of Fame, a neat river walk along the Brazos River, Cameron Park Zoo, and Fort Fisher. With so much to see and do, it's hard to be bored in Waco.

Fort Fisher, originally a Texas Ranger outpost, is now a city park and includes a nice RV park, with over 100 sites, at very reasonable rates. With our Good Sam discount, we paid $11 for a back-in site under century old oak trees, with water and electric. For a buck more, we could have had sewer as well. The park is located next door to the Texas Ranger Museum, which made it convenient to explore the displays on legendary Texas lawmen.

After getting set up, we drove downtown to the beautiful old building that houses the post office and courthouse to mail some packages, then visited the Dr. Pepper Museum, just a few blocks away. Traffic in Waco was light, and getting around was easy in our little pickup.

The nice folks at the Dr. Pepper Museum made us welcome, and Barry Wallace gave us a personal guided tour, explaining all of the displays and telling us about the history of the company and the old building that once housed the bottling plant and is now the museum.

By mid-afternoon our stomachs were growling, and just about the time Miss Terry told me we had better be thinking about food, we stumbled on Buzzard Billy's Armadillo Bar and Grill. Located in a nondescript building close to the Brazos Riverwalk, Buzzard Billy's looks like you'd think a place named Buzzard

Meandering Down The Highway

Billy's should look. An old 1960s Ford police car was parked out front, and inside were hardwood floors, an oddball assortment of decorations including antique signs and a beat up old motor scooter, and a menu full of delicious foods that had us drooling before we got past the first page.

This is no Denny's or Village Inn. If you're looking for boring food like a BLT or tuna salad, stamped out of a franchise cookie cutter, forget it. The menu at Buzzard Billy's includes such regional favorites as red beans and rice, seafood jambalaya, shrimp creole, crawfish and alligator tail. Now, I have to admit something here. I'm the world's pickiest eater. I'm allergic to onions, I hate vegetables, and I believe junk food is the nectar of the gods. All you have to do to make me happy is serve me fried dead meat, with a side of fried potatoes. My idea of ethnic food is pepperoni pizza, and to me a formal dinner is meat, potatoes and gravy. My decidedly better half, on the other hand, is a marvelous and inventive cook who gets frustrated trying to create memorable meals for a man who never strays far from meat and potatoes. But at Buzzard Billy's we met on common ground. I was feeling exotic, so we started off with Cajun popcorn, crawfish tails battered and deep fried, and served with cocktail sauce. They were delicious! For my main course, I had to try the fried alligator strips. I'd like to say that alligator tastes like chicken (chicken with really bad breath and big teeth!), but actually it was pretty bland. But who could pass up the opportunity to eat gator, right? Miss Terry had the Cajun sampler, a huge platter heaped with blackened catfish, seafood gumbo, and an order of ham and sausage jambalaya. It was just spicy enough to be interesting, but not overpowering, and we were both stuffed by the time we finished our meals. The next time you're in Waco, you really need to try Buzzard Billy's. We're glad we found the place, and we'll be back.

Meandering Down The Highway

One interesting feature in Waco is the Old Suspension Bridge across the Brazos River. Built in 1870 as a private toll bridge, this was the first span across the Brazos, and served cowboys herding cattle along the Chisholm Trail. One of the first suspension bridges in America, and at one time the longest in the world, today the bridge is closed to vehicle traffic, and pedestrians stroll leisurely across the river and pause to enjoy surrounding Indian Spring Park.

Fort Fisher is sandwiched between the Brazos River and an old cemetery, and our site faced the neat old graveyard, with its ancient headstones. Some people might be uncomfortable about parking next to such a place, but our neighbors across the wrought iron fence were quiet, which is better than I can say about some of the folks we've camped next to. Actually, we really enjoy wandering through old cemeteries and reading the inscriptions on the headstones. The next time you're feeling all upset because the car needs overhauled and your kids are being typical teenagers, take an hour or so and wander through an old cemetery. Reading the names of people who lived and died a hundred or more years ago sort of puts our daily troubles and annoyances into perspective.

We really liked Waco, and it's on our list of places to return to. Among the many other interesting sites we didn't get the chance to check out were the Governor Bill and Vera Daniel Historic Village, the natural habitat Cameron Park Zoo, the Armstrong Browning Library (housing the world's largest collection of materials relating to Robert and Elizabeth Barrett Browning), and the Strecker Museum. Everybody we met in Waco was friendly and went out of their way to make our visit enjoyable, from the checkout clerks in the stores to the folks at the Chamber of Commerce, to the jail guard we stopped to ask directions. Those folks have hospitality down to a science.

Christmas Cheer

Meandering Down The Highway

We're not really Christmas people. With our kids grown, we've become more and more disillusioned with all of the commercialism. But after much badgering from me, Miss Terry finally watched one Visa commercial too many and got with the spirit of things. She said for Christmas she wanted to be spoiled with something ridiculously expensive and that she had absolutely no need for. Now if I can just figure out how to get an iron lung into our motorhome.

We returned to Rainbow's End on Thursday, December 23rd to spend Christmas with the Escapees. When I went into the office to register, there were the welcoming hugs SKPs greet each other with, and as we were driving to our site, Hobie and Barb Hobart stopped us to welcome us back. As I've said before, the Escapees are one big extended family, and it was nice to be home.

This was our first Christmas on the road, and Rainbow's End held a big dinner in the activity center. Miss Terry is just about the best cook that ever lived, and she pitched in to help with the turkeys Christmas morning. She also made one of her delicious apple pies, with its huge golden brown crust mounded up ten inches or more over the pie pan. Everyone oohed and aahed as we carried it into the dinner, and my pretty lady sure was a big hit. People from other tables were coming over to see her creation and comment on it. Terry's rather shy, but as we've traveled and met so many wonderful people, she's becoming more comfortable meeting everyone and getting more confident. As if a lady as beautiful, intelligent and charming as mine ever had any reason not to be.

Christmas dinner was a complete success, and we had a wonderful time. Everyone came away from their tables stuffed, and the good cheer really reflected the Christmas spirit. We returned to our rig very satisfied with our first Christmas as gypsies.

The next day, the Escapees met again in the activity center

Meandering Down The Highway

for a pot luck to finish off all the leftovers. I think I'd be safe in saying we all needed to walk off a few extra pounds before the weekend was over.

Closing Out The Twentieth Century

We were working hard to get this edition wrapped up as the year drew to a close, but found that it wasn't an easy task. Every day at Rainbow's End we found ourselves entertaining visitors who dropped by the rig to subscribe to the *Gypsy Journal* or just to say hello, and when we'd walk over to pick up our mail, we'd be invited into someone else's RV and before we knew it, an hour or two was gone in pleasant conversation. Not that we're complaining at all - it was like being part of one big happy family, with everyone in a holiday mood. Several of our new friends offered to take bundles of the newspapers to the different RV parks they were heading for after the holidays, greatly increasing our exposure. We really appreciate so many new friends and supporters pitching in to help us reach new readers. It goes a long way toward expanding our subscription list.

More of that small world syndrome kicked in while we were at Rainbow's End. We had gone into Livingston to run a few errands one day, and when we returned to the park, new neighbors had moved into the site next to us. Before we were even out of the pickup, John and Mary Marschalk came out to greet us. It seems they had picked up a copy of the *Gypsy Journal* earlier in their travels and had decided to subscribe. John said Mary was just sitting down to write the check when they glanced out their window and saw our truck, with the newspaper's name on the sides, pull in beside them. The same day, Rick and Laurie Phillips dropped by the rig. They had been at the outlet mall in Conroe a couple of weeks earlier and parked next to our truck. Laurie said they wondered what the *Gypsy Journal* was and waited for us to return to our truck for a while (we were off in a bookstore, where we tend to get lost for hours at a time) and finally gave up. Now

Meandering Down The Highway

they were at Rainbow's End and saw us again! Rick and Laurie are wonderful folks and they gave us a grand tour of their beautiful Safari Serengeti coach. We're heading in the same general direction after the first of the year, and hope we'll meet up again soon.

Our only concession to the Y2K hoopla was to fill our gasoline, propane and fresh water tanks. Then we headed over to the activity center for a great New Year's Eve party. There was good food, good conversation, and that pretty lady of mine and I even managed to drag ourselves away from it all to take a turn or two around the dance floor.

Our table included Jim and Natalie Chatham, and Bob and Natalie Aikens. Though we had never met either couple when we sat down, within a few minutes we were chatting away with our new friends and having a fine time. As it turns out, Jim is a massage therapist, and the next day he spent a couple of hours working all the kinks and knots out of our muscles. By the time he was finished, Terry and I both felt like a couple of lumps of clay, it was so relaxing. Jim and Natalie have a gorgeous Dutch Star diesel rig, and they gave us the grand tour. I was hoping Santa might have left us a new diesel rig, but maybe he's holding out for our anniversary in January.

Well, the New Year is here, and none of the doomsayers' predictions proved true. No airplanes fell out of the sky, the lights stayed on, this old world kept on turning, and we're off in search of new adventures. We'll be heading further east along the Gulf coast in the next few weeks. Since Miss Terry finally gave in and allowed me to get one of those maps for the side of our motorhome to record our journeys on, we've got lots of states to fill in. I've wanted to visit New Orleans forever, we want to explore Cajun country a little bit, and who knows where we'll end up? That's the great thing about our life on the road - there's always something new to see just down the road and around the

Meandering Down The Highway

next bend. Wherever the road takes us, we know it'll be interesting, and there'll be new friends to meet and places to tell you about. Until next time, hope to see you in our travels.

Meandering Down The Highway

March-April, 2000

We had been in Livingston, Texas at the Escapees Rainbow's End park for a couple of weeks over the holidays, and had a bad case of hitch itch. We had the January-February issue of the *Gypsy Journal* printed in Huntsville, and as soon as the mailing envelopes were stuffed, we hit the road Friday morning, January 7.

Highway 190 east of Livingston to the Louisiana border ranged from wide four lane to narrow two lane. In Newton, Texas the county courthouse sitting in the town square caught our attention. A gorgeous old building that would make any architectural fan stop for a second look, the stately old building really gives the town character. Newton appeared to be a clean little town, and fairly prosperous.

The topography of eastern Texas as we approached the state line became swampy as it transformed to bayou country. Just east of Bon Weir we passed Quicksand Creek, where Miss Terry wanted me to go wading for some strange reason. Just past the creek we crossed the Sabin River into Boureaguard Parish, Louisiana.

Louisiana Back Roads

Even in early January, there was a tremendous amount of green in the countryside in Louisiana. We had been disappointed to see how much litter there was in parts of east Texas and the many rundown houses sitting alongside the roadways, but Louisiana was much cleaner. The roadsides looked neater, and even the houses in the small towns we passed through seemed

Meandering Down The Highway

more tidy. We chose Highway 190 to cross Louisiana because we had heard horror stories about Interstate 10. Highway 190 had the occasional rough spot, but overall provided a nice ride, taking us through several small towns.

In Eunice we stopped at a grocery store to pick up some sandwich materials, then had lunch in the parking lot. Near Opelousas the highway took us through several bayous, the water under the bridges covered with algae. It was too late in the day to stop and tour the Jim Bowie Museum in Opelousas, so we had to mark it down on our places to visit later calendar.

East of Opelousas the highway got rough for a bit, and we crossed a bayou on a long, narrow bridge. We met a semi pulling a wide load on the bridge, and for a few brief seconds wondered if we were going to make it through without scraping, but squeezed by with a few inches to spare.

At Baton Rouge we crossed the Mississippi River. Terry spotted a tugboat pushing two barges on the water below us. We hit Baton Rouge at 4:30 in the afternoon, but traffic wasn't bad and we rolled through without delay.

Picking up Interstate 12 at Baton Rouge, we promptly hit a road block for construction that had us creeping along in stop and go traffic for the next 45 minutes. Terry started cataloguing the litter alongside the highway at one stop and came up with an eclectic list, including a dashboard cover, a full roll of toilet paper (I don't know, don't ask), a 2x4, several hubcaps, a shirt, and assorted trash. I have never understood why people litter at all, but even then, it's harder to figure out why they throw away some of the things they do. Was the shirt too small? The wrong color? Did someone replace their wardrobe for the New Millennium? As for whomever threw away the toilet paper, some day you're really going to need it and wish you had it back.

I will say that Louisiana people are friendly, though. While we were stopped in the traffic jam, a couple of good old boys in

Meandering Down The Highway

the truck in the lane next to us offered me a beer. I hated to turn down their southern hospitality, but I don't drink, so I had to decline. At several places in Louisiana and Mississippi we saw roadside vendors peddling hot boiled peanuts, which are apparently a local delicacy.

We stopped for the night at Western Horizon's Abita Springs Resort, on the north side of Lake Ponchetrain. Someone at the Escapee park in Livingston had provided us with a hand drawn map to Abita Springs, but either we missed a turn or their cartography wasn't too good, because we ended up driving down a narrow two lane road through miles of forest in the dark. Miss Terry was driving, while I searched vainly for any sign of civilization or a place big enough to turn around. Scenes from the old movie *Deliverance* began to roll through my mind as I pictured tobacco chewing backwoodsmen violating the things I treasure most while an inbred banjo player plucked out a manic tune. Eventually we spotted a small airport and managed to get turned around and headed back to the land of fast food and indoor plumbing.

Southern Sights

We spent the night at Abita Springs, then headed out again the next morning to pay a visit to Ray Fernandez at Passport America in Long Beach, Mississippi. The Mississippi Welcome Center on Interstate 10 really impressed us. Set in a plantation style building, filled with period antiques and boasting a beautiful spiral staircase that had us thinking about Tara and Scarlett O'Hara, the Welcome Center was staffed by several friendly young ladies who offered us free Coca Cola and were eager to answer any questions we had. The Welcome Center/rest area was just beautiful, a huge park-like area with trees, picnic tables, and a dump station. Mississippi has similar welcome centers on all of the major highways coming into the state. This is one state that wants visitors to feel welcome, and their goodwill ambassadors at

Meandering Down The Highway

the Welcome Centers certainly do a fine job. It's worth driving to Mississippi just to stop at the Welcome Center. We noted a sign at the Welcome Center telling us that Interstate 10 through Mississippi is the Vietnam Veterans Memorial Highway.

We dropped down to Highway 90 along the Gulf Coast, where white beaches lined one side of the roadway, while beautiful old houses faced the water from the other side. In Waveland I saw an advertisement on a bus stop bench for a minister available for weddings at your location. Who says commercialism has gone too far? Another sign that caught my eye, in front of a church in Long Beach, said the three enemies of joy are hurry, worry and doubt.

Passport America had contacted us a few weeks earlier with an offer to distribute sample copies of the *Gypsy Journal* at RV shows around the country, as well as in the packets that go out to their new members.

Ray Fernandez, Passport America's president, is a friendly man who really made us feel welcome, even offering to put us up at his Magic River Resort for a few days. We had a commitment down the road, but promised to stop back in a week or so. We've used Passport America member parks several times in our travels, and found them to be very good values. With a lower membership cost than any other camping organization we've come across, and hundreds of member parks all over the country, you can save enough to recoup your $39 membership fee (since increased to $44) in just a week on the road. Ray, Tiffany Ingram, and Brent in the company's office treated us like family, giving me the run of the place to check my e-mail every day, get a fax sent in, and use the telephone. The company may service thousands of members in the course of a week, but they've never lost their down-home family way of doing business. We left several thousand copies of the *Gypsy Journal* for them to distribute, agreed on an advertising program, and Ray even handed us a stack of membership cards

Meandering Down The Highway

and campground directories so we could sign up new members for him - all on just a handshake. These are my kind of people.

After we left Long Beach we connected with Interstate 10 again and crossed into Alabama. In Mobile the highway drops down into a tunnel to take you under the downtown area, climbs back out again in time to give you a view of the battleship *Alabama*, then crosses over a long causeway across Mobile Bay.

We arrived at the Rainbow Plantation, the Escapees park in Summerdale, Alabama at about 5:30 p.m., and our friends Rick and Laurie Phillips met us at the registration office with warm welcoming hugs. Our site was just a few spaces away from where they had their Safari set up. It's always fun to meet new people as we travel, but there sure is something comforting about pulling into a strange place and seeing familiar, friendly faces. Our friends helped us get set up, then we all clomped inside our rig to compare notes on our recent travels and the places we had camped.

Rainbow Plantation is a very pretty park, with huge spaces, a large club house, and the friendly Escapee family atmosphere we love so much. The temperature was comfortable, but the humidity was so high it seemed like you could reach out and grab a handful of the moist air. Terry and I agreed that while we liked the area in the winter, we probably wouldn't want to spend much time here in the summer when the temperature soars. I imagine it might be much like a sauna.

The evening after our arrival, at the Sunday Social Hour at Rainbow Plantation, the park's assistant manager gave the *Gypsy Journal* a glowing endorsement, saying that in his opinion it provided more real RVing information than *Highways*, *Trailer Life* or *Motorhome* magazines. I have to admit that my head swelled just a little bit at the praise, okay, it swelled *a lot*! Miss Terry had to hold onto my belt to keep me anchored in my seat. I was about to float up toward the ceiling. While at the Social Hour,

Meandering Down The Highway

we ran into RV columnists Bill Farlow, who has a lot at Rainbow Plantation, and Joe and Vicki Kieva, who were on their way to speaking engagements at the big Tampa, Florida RV show.

The sky had been overcast all day, and Sunday night the rain began to pour. The *Weather Channel* was reporting a tornado watch all along the Gulf Coast, and about midnight the wind came up so strong it wasn't hard to imagine a twister or two barreling through. But by morning the storm had blown itself out, and Monday was gorgeous.

Tuesday we left the RV at the Plantation and drove our pickup to Pensacola, Florida to visit the National Museum of Naval Aviation at Naval Air Station Pensacola. Entering Florida on Highway 98, there are several signs telling you about all of the ways you can get into trouble on the state's highways. *Seatbelt Laws Strictly Enforced*, *Speed Laws Enforced*, *Children Must Be In A Child Restraint*, *$500 Fine For Littering*, and a couple of others. I agree with all of those laws, but it was kind of intimidating to be hit with one warning sign after another. You can bet I behaved all the time we were there!

We've visited a lot of museums in our travels, but nothing we've seen compares to this collection of aircraft and exhibits relating to Naval aviation. Every kind of aircraft from World War I biplanes to jet fighters that saw action in Desert Storm is parked on the museum's floor or hanging from the ceiling. We spent six hours at the museum and never saw all of it.

Our tour guide, Huntley Johnson, is a former Marine pilot who flew torpedo bombers in the South Pacific during World War II and was called back to duty during the Korean War. Flying out of Bougainville, in the Solomon Islands in 1943, Huntley was shot down, but he and his two crewmen survived and were later plucked off a life raft to fight again. Huntley said that during the action, legendary pilot Joe Foss was flying cover over his flight. During his time in uniform Huntley flew Avengers, Corsairs, and

Meandering Down The Highway

served as an instructor pilot at Pensacola. Huntley is now an investment counselor, and volunteers at the museum. It's obvious he's proud of his work, and during our tour he shared several war stories and bits of inside information about many of the different aircraft on display. If you have any interest at all in old warplanes and their part in our history, this is one place you don't want to miss. But when you go, plan to spend at least an entire day, because you'll need it.

We learned that on Interstate 10 in the Florida Panhandle, the exit numbers are not keyed to the mile markers. We were out dropping off sample copies of the *Gypsy Journal*, and east of Pensacola, the exits are miles apart, though they're numbered sequentially. Why don't at least the Interstate highways follow some uniform numbering system? Florida and California both seem to go their own way, instead of using the system other states do - keying their exit numbers to mile marker numbers.

For a short period when she was a youngster, Miss Terry had lived in Fort Walton Beach, Florida. We drove to the city to see if we could locate anything that might trigger a memory from so long ago, but whatever buildings had existed at that time were buried under tons of concrete and asphalt as high rise hotels and condominiums conquered the coast. Along the way we stopped at several RV resorts to drop off sample copies. Everywhere we've ever visited, RV park owners and managers have been happy to have sample copies to give to their guests. Everyone wins with our samples - the resorts get something to give to their guests at no cost to them, the RVers get a free newspaper, and we get quite a few subscribers out of the deal. For the first time, we ran into a park manager who didn't want us to leave any papers. The fellow at one resort on Highway 98 must have been having a bad day, and he let me know it. I asked if I could leave a few sample copies of the *Gypsy Journal*, and he told me that every inch of his property cost him money, and he was NOT going to use any of it to display

Meandering Down The Highway

our newspapers. I suggested that many RV parks find that their guests really appreciate finding the *Gypsy Journal*, and his reply was that his guests never stayed around long enough for him to care what they appreciated. Gee, go figure. When I get to feeling that way, I find that a bran muffin and a cup of coffee usually clears up my disposition right away.

We spent another day exploring the Eastern Shore area of Baldwin County, Alabama. Flo, at the Tourist Welcome Center in Spanish Fort was very helpful, loading us down with a ton of brochures and tips about places to visit locally. Wherever your RVing adventures take you, you can always find lots of interesting places to visit and historical locations to discover.

One of the best things about RVing is the many great people we meet, both in and out of RV parks. So often, when people in the places we visit learn that we live and travel fulltime in our motorhome, they tell us they wish they could live the lifestyle. What they don't understand is that they *can* enjoy the freedom of fulltiming. Anyone who is willing to work at it can fulltime. We've met families with children who home school them on the road. We, and many other baby boomer fulltimers, earn our living on the road as we travel. We've met many older fulltimers who travel alone, including Lee Snow, an 83 year old woman traveling solo who has been living the fulltime lifestyle for 34 years! We've met physically handicapped RVers, those who need to arrange for dialysis as they travel, a couple who travel with elderly parents, many whose budgets would only fit in the purchase of fifteen or twenty year old RVs - they're all out here sharing the road and the lifestyle. Now tell me again, why you can't enjoy this freedom too?

One day's exploration took us down to Gulf Shores, on the coast. After wandering around town a bit, we drove out to Fort Morgan, a Civil War fort that helped protect the entrance to Mobile Bay. It was here that Admiral David Farragaut,

Meandering Down The Highway

commander of the Union fleet attacking Mobile, shouted the famous order that we all learned in history class, *"Damn the torpedoes, full speed ahead!"* For more on Fort Morgan, look for the feature story in this issue.

From Fort Morgan, we took the ferry across the bay to Daulphin Island, and spent several hours wandering around the waterfront and exploring the island's back roads. Crossing the bridge from the island back to the mainland, we had a nice seafood meal at the Pier Four Restaurant. Our table afforded us a great view of the battleship *Alabama* and the sunset over the bay, and the food was wonderful.

Miss Terry and I celebrated our second wedding anniversary January 16 by driving north to Fort Mims, site of the largest Indian led massacre in America. Driving down the back road that leads to Fort Mims, we passed a cluster of shacks and run down mobile homes, coon dogs and ragged kids playing around the junker cars in the yards. I swear I spotted comedian Jeff Foxworthy taking notes for his next *You Might Be A Redneck* routine. On our way back to Rainbow Plantation we stopped at a small flea market to check out the bargains. Who says I don't know how to show a lady a good time on a special day?

Mansions and Beaches

Monday, January 17, we rolled up our awnings and said a reluctant goodby to Rainbow Plantation and the friends we made there, returning to Long Beach, Mississippi and Passport America's Magic River resort. I pulled a dumb stunt on the way back to Long Beach and got away with it, but learned a lesson. Gasoline in Alabama cost about six or seven cents a gallon more than we paid in Mississippi, so even though our fuel gauge was reading low, I decided to wait until we arrived at the Flying J on Interstate 10 in Mississippi to gas up. Though the distance from Rainbow Plantation to the truck stop is only a little over 100 miles, those miles sure seemed long, and the needle was solidly

Meandering Down The Highway

parked on E when we finally pulled up to the truck stop's RV fuel island. Our motorhome has a 75 gallon gas tank, and when I got done filling it, the pump told me I had poured in 74.75 gallons! With only a quart of gas left, I figure we could have made it about another mile or so, if the road was flat enough and we had a strong tailwind. I made Miss Terry promise to slap me upside my head the next time I let our tank get under 1/4 full.

Ray Fernandez and the crew at Passport America really made us feel welcome when we returned, and we parked the rig in one of their sites to spend a few days getting to know this special corner of the world. For some silly reason I never thought of Mississippi as a coastal state, even though I remember getting an A in fifth grade geography class. Come to think of it, I think I copied my test answers from that pretty red headed girl who sat next to me. But though Mississippi's coastline isn't very long, it sure packs in a lot of beauty and history in a minimal number of miles. The coast has been a resort area since early settlement days, when wealthy plantation owners from other parts of the south came here to build elaborate summer homes to escape the heat and diseases back home. Today many of those summer homes remain, huge mansions that left us gaping in awe at their size and beauty. While most are private homes, several have been turned into bed and breakfasts, giving the rest of us the opportunity to book a reservation and have a chance to see how the other half lives. With today's modern highways and airports making transportation to the area even easier, and with the addition of such attractions as museums, casinos, charter fishing and golf courses, the coast is even more popular today.

We learned a lot of neat things while staying at Magic River, including being introduced to nutria and King Cake. The resort has two small fishing ponds, and one evening Miss Terry and I took a stroll around them just at sunset. Several ducks winter on the ponds, and while we were watching them, I spotted something

Meandering Down The Highway

swimming in the pond. It turned out to be a pair of nutria, otter-like critters who live on a small island in the pond and spend their evenings frolicking in the water. The locals call them nutrarats, and depending on who you talk to, they're either cute or repulsive. Everyone seemed to be in agreement that King Cake is much more appealing than nutria. King Cake is a Mardi Gras tradition anywhere along the coast. A colorfully decorated coffeecake sort of pastry, it's eaten in the weeks leading up to the Mardi Gras celebration. Each cake contains a small baby doll, and whoever gets the piece with the baby is King for the Day. There's a downside though, the honor comes with the obligation of buying the next day's King Cake. By the way, did you know that Mardi Gras isn't celebrated only in New Orleans? Quite a few other communities throughout the region have their own Mardi Gras parades and parties, on a smaller scale.

Getting To Know New Orleans

I've always thought of New Orleans as one of the most romantic cities in America, even though the only opportunity I ever had to visit was back when I was a young soldier, when myself and a couple of other GIs spent an evening there. Back then we were too busy trying to act grown up as we gawked at the sinful sights of Bourbon Street to appreciate the city's culture and beauty. I've wanted to get back ever since.

It's only a little over an hour's drive from Magic River to New Orleans, so on Friday we left the RV at the resort and drove into the Crescent City for the day. (Did you know New Orleans is called the Crescent City because of the shape of the land it occupies at the mouth of the Mississippi River? Isn't it amazing how much information you get in just one issue of the *Gypsy Journal*? Now remember, if you use this tidbit of knowledge to win a million bucks on some quiz show, I get a new diesel motorhome out of the deal, okay?) Over the years I've been in most of the major cities in the country. Some were memorable,

Meandering Down The Highway

others just huge concrete jungles. But no place I have ever visited has its own personality like New Orleans. It struck a chord deep in my soul.

We knew we didn't have enough time to see everything, or to even scratch the surface of all that this magical place has to offer, so we chose to confine our explorations this trip to the French Quarter.

Ask a hundred different people their opinions of the French Quarter, and you'll probably get a hundred different answers. Some will tell you it's the most exciting place they've ever been. Others will be turned off by its character. Some will say they can't wait to get back again, while others will declare that they never want to set foot in the place again. They'll all be right.

The most ancient part of the city, the French Quarter is gaudy, tacky, dirty, irreverent, and eccentric. It's also charming, funny, lovable, quirky and sad. Here you'll find buildings dating back 250 years or more, once homes to slave traders, pirates, generals, explorers, and merchants, that today house funky shops selling Mardi Gras masks and beads, T-shirts and cigars. Where antebellum ladies once attended formal balls in their finest silk gowns, today you'll see an eclectic mixture of tourists and locals doing their own thing, whatever that may be.

They call New Orleans the Big Easy, a reference to the city's laid back acceptance of whatever works for you, and when does the party start? It may not be right for you, but I like it. In the course of our day in the French Quarter we walked for miles down her narrow streets, browsed through a wonderful marketplace, watched every kind of street performer you can imagine, and I even got the chance to fulfill a long held dream, a visit to singer/songwriter Jimmy Buffett's Margaritaville Cafe, where Miss Terry and I stuffed ourselves on Cheeseburgers in Paradise. Along the way we paused to clap along with the rest of the crowd keeping time to the music of a Dixieland band in Jackson Square

Meandering Down The Highway

playing *When the Saints Go Marching In*, played paparazzi by snapping a couple of photographs of Vanna White as they taped some background shots for television's *Wheel of Fortune*, marveled over the beautiful architecture of the old buildings, got hustled by a street-wise con man and drank in the sights, sounds, smells and sensations of this wonderful, wacky city. I couldn't live in New Orleans, it takes too much energy. But I can promise you that I'll return again and again.

Moving On

We had originally planned to drive up to Red Bay, Alabama and tour the Allegro factory, but a winter storm was dumping snow throughout the southeast, so we decided to head west in search of warmer temperatures. We left Magic River just after noon on Saturday, January 22 with heavy clouds hanging low in the sky. Skirting the north end of Lake Pontchartrain on Interstate 12, we rolled across Louisiana. As we passed a rest area on the eastern edge of Louisiana, Miss Terry had spotted a gorgeous old pickup pulling a teardrop camper, but I was too busy doing battle with a monster tractor-trailer rig on the highway to look before we were past it.

But west of Baton Rogue the gleaming black 1937 Chevy pickup pulled up beside us and the driver honked and waved. "Darn, I wish he'd pull into that rest area up ahead," I told Terry as the truck pulled away from us. "I'd love to get a better look at that outfit." "Well, I doubt it," she replied, "He was in that rest area a while back. He probably won't be stopping anytime soon." As if on cue, the trailer's turn signal came on and the old truck pulled into the rest area up ahead. We followed it in and got out to say hello.

Bill Umberger, of Edwardsville, Illinois, told us his son had started the restoration of the truck, but passed away before it was completed. Bill finished the job, and then built the old-fashioned tiny teardrop trailer from scratch. What a beautiful creation!

Meandering Down The Highway

We've been classic car nuts forever, and that old pickup was as nice as anything I've seen anywhere. The trailer is the perfect complement, looking just like the old teardrops that were among the first RVs. Bill told us the trailer isn't just a toy, he actually sleeps in it when he's on a trip. Now, that's traveling in style!

People keep telling us that Interstate 10 through Louisiana is a terrible stretch of road, so we were a little apprehensive about what to expect. I can't say it's the smoothest route I've ever driven, but in my opinion, it's not nearly as bad as Interstate 40 eastbound through New Mexico. Now *that's* an axle buster! Interstate 10 was bumpy enough, with some pretty rough potholes but we bounced along just fine, crossing over bayous that stretched on for miles. Between fighting the steering wheel when semi's buffeted us and dodging kamikaze drivers in family sedans and mini vans, I tried to glance out now and then in hopes of spotting an alligator, but the closest thing I saw was a middle-aged lady from Minnesota who was glaring at me as their Dodge Caravan roared past because I wouldn't climb the guardrail to give them a lane and a half. A little after 5 p.m. we were out of the bad weather and stopped for the night at the Jean Lafitte RV Park in Lake Charles, Louisiana. We had covered 250 miles, much of it in intermittent showers and on wet roads, more than enough for one day.

Sometime during the night a hard rainstorm hit the RV park, rain pounding the RV and pouring in through the vents and windows we had left open to fight the humid heat. The first order of business when we woke up Sunday morning was to wipe up the mess.

We crossed into Texas and pulled into the Flying J at Beaumont to fuel up and fill our propane tank, then took Highway 90 over to Route 146 and were back at Rainbow's End in Livingston shortly after noon. What a difference in the Escapee park since our visit over the holidays! Then the place was

Meandering Down The Highway

crowded, and RVs were packed in so close together you could hear the furnace and water heater in the next rig come on. The park still had quite a few rigs, but nowhere near as full.

We arrived under sunny skies with temperatures in the mid-70s, but the bad weather we had been dealing with further east soon closed in, and for the two days we were at Livingston, clouds blanketed the sky and the temperature stayed in the 40s. Compared to the weather they were experiencing back in the southeast, we didn't have it all that bad. Alabama, Georgia, and the Carolinas were all experiencing snow and freezing rain.

Winter Storm

Wednesday, January 26, we left Livingston and took Interstate 45 north out of Huntsville to Dallas, where we hooked up with Interstate 20 heading east. I had been dreading the traffic in the Dallas - Fort Worth metro area, but Interstate 20 took us south of most of the urban area, and we zipped right through and out into the high plains.

Early in the afternoon the clouds started spitting rain and the wind picked up. We had planned to spend the night in Midland or Odessa, but as the weather deteriorated, we started thinking about finding a campground in Sweetwater. Those plans changed as the wind grew stronger, and when Miss Terry spotted a sign for White's RV Park in Clyde, Texas, we pulled in for the night. By the time we registered and Irene White got us into our pull-through site, it was downright cold, and the wind seemed to cut through me as I hooked up to water and electric. Since we were only staying for the night, and my pudgy little fingers were beginning to freeze, I didn't bother with the sewer connection. You gotta love those holding tanks!

White's is a small park, maybe 30 or so spaces, and very clean. Irene gave us a discount since we were Escapees, and we left a stack of newspapers for her to pass out. We'd have liked to visit with her more, but we were just too worn out from our rough

Meandering Down The Highway

day on the road.

All night long the wind rocked our rig, and when we woke up Thursday morning everything was coated in ice. Stepping outside, I slid on ice-coated steps and bruised my dignity, then had to fight to get the frozen door of our pickup open. When we cranked in our slide rooms, great sheets of ice fell off and crashed to the ground like panes of glass. I walked up to the office, where a fellow RVer was talking on a CB radio with truckers out on the interstate. They reported that within 30 miles or so west, the road was clear and dry, but that to the east it was terrible.

We decided to hit the road, figuring that in not much more than a half hour or so we'd be in the clear. Bad decision. If we could have gotten underway right away, we might have been okay. But our wonderful Pace Arrow decided to remind us just why it's the Motorhome from Hell, and when I tried to raise the hydraulic jacks they wouldn't work. Checking, I discovered we apparently have another leak, because the fluid reservoir for our slide rooms was empty again. The mechanics insist the jack and slide systems are completely separate, but no one can explain to me why, when I fill the slide out reservoir, our jacks start working again.

We got the jacks up, but the alarm started beeping every time I took off the emergency brake. Checking to be sure the jacks were up, we knew it was the sensor. Finally we did what everyone must resort to sooner or later, we called Dad. I remembered that Miss Terry's father, Pete Weber, had once had the same problem with his Pace Arrow. Pete told us he had disconnected the sensor until he could get it repaired, and told us how to do it. Two hours later than we had planned on, we finally got out on the highway, and quickly wished we had stayed put.

The road was slippery, but we held our speed down and managed all right. We spotted a couple of big rigs flipped on their sides, and wondered at the stupidity of other drivers who roared

Meandering Down The Highway

past us at high speed, endangering themselves and everyone near them. The 30 miles of bad weather we had expected stretched out to 50, then 75, then 100. Finally, several hours and about 150 miles later we broke into the clear and pulled into the Escapees Trapark RV Park at Pecos, Texas. I made Miss Terry promise to box my ears the next time I decided to "drive out" of a storm. It was a foolish choice when we were in a safe park and hooked up to services. We live and learn, and hopefully, survive along the way.

Oil, Wind and Cattle

I'm amazed at the differences from one part of Texas to another. In the south you have a beautiful coastline, the central portion has lovely rolling hills, and east Texas is covered with pine trees and has some marvelous lakes. But I still don't know why anyone bothered to settle in west Texas. The mostly flat, barren landscape seems to go on forever, broken up here and there by oil pumps and a few head of cattle leaning into the wind. People can see beauty in many things, but I'm sorry, I just can't find any reason to become fond of west Texas.

Pecos sits atop the Permian Basin, an oil-rich reserve that has made many speculators filthy rich for decades, while it left others just broke and filthy. Next to the RV park is Maxey Park and Zoo, where a few decrepit animals sit around being as bored as the local people. We wanted to stop by the West of the Pecos Museum, which several people have told us about, but it was just too cold to get enthused about much of anything. We enjoyed visiting with the staff at the park, but by the next morning we were more than ready to hit the road.

The sky was still grey, and we ran into some fog, but as we moved west it thinned, and about the time we hit Interstate 10 we were under blue sky, though it was still cold. The sagebrush alongside the highway carried a heavy coating of frost even in the middle of the day, looking very pretty, but sending a visual chill

Meandering Down The Highway

through us.

About fifty miles east of El Paso the wind picked up again, throwing us around the highway and making for white knuckle driving. The RV Consumers Group rates our Pace Arrow Vision as unsafe on the highway, and all you have to do is drive it a few miles on a windy day to understand why. While other RVs may be buffeted by gusts, our model is prone to change lanes if we're driving at speeds over 50 miles per hour.

Traffic in El Paso was heavy, but with Miss Terry's sharp eyes helping me navigate, we got through it just fine. Coming into the city, we spotted an eighteen wheeler pulled over and surrounded by police cars, it's rear doors hanging open. We speculated about what was going on. Was it someone caught smuggling illegal aliens or a load of drugs?

I can't understand why gasoline prices in west Texas are so high, with all of the area's oil reserves. We saw some gas station signs advertising prices of $1.50 a gallon, while back in Livingston, it was going for $1.16. When we passed through El Paso in November, we paid $1.16 at Flying J, this trip the cost was $1.24.

Retracing Earlier Routes

With El Paso behind us, we headed for Dream Catcher RV Park in Deming, New Mexico. The ninety miles or so into Deming were a constant battle with the wind. As Interstate 10 took a more westerly heading, the cross wind changed to head-on, making driving somewhat easier, even if it took a toll on our gas mileage. Arriving at Dream Catcher in the middle of social hour Friday afternoon, we visited a bit, then got the RV set up on our site and said a silent thank you to whatever guardian angel looks after RVers and other gypsies for getting us there safe and sound through all the bad weather and heavy traffic.

When we came through Deming in November, Dream Catcher had quite a few RVs in the park, but now, in late January

Meandering Down The Highway

the place was packed. We made several new friends at Dream catcher, and ran into some we had met earlier. Ike and Marty Morgan, on their way back to seasonal jobs driving shuttle buses at the Grand Canyon, were next to us in their Winnebago. Ike has had quite a few problems with his RV's fuel pump, so we compared notes and tried to decide which of us liked our rigs less. It was nice to meet Ike and Marty, and we promised to stop by and visit them at the Grand Canyon sometime during our travels.

We drove down to Columbus, New Mexico on Saturday to look around. Colombus earned its place in history back in 1916, when Mexican revolutionaries led by Pancho Villa raided the town, killing several civilians, as well as some soldiers stationed in the town. The local historical society museum has an interesting collection of items relating to the raid, and Pancho Villa State Park, just across the street, also has a small museum in its visitor center. Columbus is a sleepy, rather run down little town, but everyone we met was friendly and seemed happy there.

Deming is another friendly town that seems to cater to RVers. A lot of snowbirds seem to prefer Deming over somewhat warmer, but more crowded roosts such as Tucson and Phoenix. Most of the RV parks we saw were pretty well filled up. At the Furr's Grocery Store, Miss Terry was delighted to find a section well stocked with hard to find exotic ethnic spices that really put a gleam in her chef's eye.

Sunday morning we made ready to leave Deming, and I raised a few eyebrows in the RV park when someone in the office asked me how I could possibly plan on traveling on Super Bowl Sunday. I told them I'm not into baseball. A fellow spoke up and told me the Super Bowl is a football game. That's when I replied that I stopped following the game when Billy Jean King and Bobby Riggs had their silly go-around back in the 70's. When some people learn I have absolutely no interest in sports, aside from watching a stock car race or boxing match once or twice a

Meandering Down The Highway

decade, they look at me like I must be a communist. I'm sorry, I just can't get excited watching spoiled, overpaid athletes scratching themselves on television. I used to really enjoy racing, and I've even climbed behind the wheel of a stock car a time or two. But really, when it comes right down to it, aside from a few nasty crashes once in a while, all you do at a race is watch red necks turn left for an hour or two.

Still fighting the wind on Interstate 10, an hour west of Deming we pulled into Steins ghost town to visit with our friends Larry and Linda Link. We featured Steins in our last issue, and Linda told us several RVers have stopped in, telling them they read about the town in the *Gypsy Journal*. Larry was out taking some folks on a tour when we arrived, but returned soon to pick up the banter where we left off on our last visit.

A couple from back east stopped into the Mercantile, and Larry was in high form. But some people just don't have a sense of humor, and these two definitely fell into that category. "This is my illegitimate brother, the writer," Larry told them, introducing me. "Mom and Dad sent him off to get an education. They kept me home to work the farm. Or was that to fatten up to butcher?" The couple frowned. "I bought the wife a new shovel for Christmas," Larry quipped, "and she's just about got it broken in." The lady's lips remained firmly clamped together, without a hint of a smile. Larry was working hard, but these folks just weren't giving him a break. I, on the other hand, was stifling a giggle and jumping in whenever Larry would let me get a word in. But these visitors just stared at us like we were a couple of performing monkeys, which probably isn't all that far from the truth. I've got to figure that if someone can't appreciate all of the comic talent on display in that historic old store that day, they're probably missing a chromosome somewhere. Their loss.

We crossed into Arizona and began the long pull uphill past

Meandering Down The Highway

Wilcox and into Texas Canyon. I've always enjoyed the rock formations in the canyon, but this trip it was all I could do to hang onto the steering wheel and try to keep the RV in one lane. The wind whipped us in huge gusts, throwing us all over the road. Outside of Tucson a few miles the wind finally decreased a bit and made driving easier.

I've lived in Tucson a couple of times, and every time I pass through I see something new. The growth all over the southwest is phenomenal, and Tucson is no exception. A couple of years ago, Pima County decided it needed a new stadium, and the bean counters who run things decided the best way to pay for it was a tax on visitors. Why make the local folks who live here pay for it, when they can make visitors who will probably never use the stadium foot the bill? (Probably because a lot of the locals know they'd never use it either?) The tax has made a decided dent in Tucson's RVer traffic as snowbirds go elsewhere to avoid what they feel is an unfair added expense, but the stubborn bureaucrats won't budge. It's a loss for everyone - I'm sure Tucson's businesses lose much more in snowbird dollars than the tax will ever bring in, and the RVers don't get the chance to spend time in a neat city that has a lot to offer visitors.

The trip from Tucson to Casa Grande was less than an hour, and we arrived at Western Horizon's Desert Shadows Resort a little before 6 p.m. This was our first time to stay at Desert Shadows, and we were very impressed with the resort's many amenities. The place was packed, and since we didn't have a reservation, they could only put us up for one night. Since we were headed for the Phoenix area, that was no problem. But in the short time we were at Desert Shadows, we sold a couple of subscriptions to folks who had picked up sample copies of the *Gypsy Journal* earlier. The next morning we drove the short distance to Gilbert, Arizona and pulled into Miss Terry's grandmother's yard, our favorite parking spot in the Phoenix

Meandering Down The Highway

area.

We really hadn't wanted to return west so soon, but unfinished business in Arizona, like the tentacles of a stubborn octopus, keep dragging us back. We still have a few items stored with family that we need to dispose of, and a couple of dangling business matters that keep popping up every time we think they're resolved. There's a lot to see and do in the West, and we could never cover it all, but we want to give our readers and ourselves a look at the rest of the country, as well. It looks like we'll be stuck spending more time in Arizona and California than we had planned on for a while yet, but our plans call for extended travels in the Midwest and east in the coming months.

After a few days in Gilbert, we saddled up and traveled to Kingman, Arizona for a brief visit with our friend Mike Howard. Then we drove over to Riverside, California to the Fleetwood factory.

There are two Highway 95s running south along the Colorado River, which forms the border between Arizona and California. Arizona State Highway 95 runs south from Interstate 40 to Interstate 10, passing through Lake Havasu City on the way. We choose U.S. Highway 95, on the California side of the river The highway climbs through some low mountains, between Needles and Blythe, and there were RVs everywhere. We saw huge Class A's, travel trailers, and fifth wheels of every description. During the winter, this is truly snowbird country.

Traveling west on Interstate 10 east of Indio, California, we spotted heavy black smoke ahead, a pretty good indication of a vehicle fire. Sure enough, we soon pulled up on a travel trailer fully engulfed in flames. I jumped out with a fire extinguisher, but it was obvious the rig was too far gone. Fortunately, no one was injured, but it was a sobering sight to see. This is the second RV fire I've seen, and they are terrible things. When these rigs burn,

Meandering Down The Highway

they burn fast. About all you can do is get yourself and your passengers clear and stand back.

The Motorhome From Hell Goes Back To the Factory

The problems with our Pace Arrow Vision have continued. Besides the earlier deficiencies I've described, which included having the hydraulic system fail and our living room slide go out while we were driving down Highway 101 in Oregon (that's an experience to write home about), having the bedroom slide fail and drop down to crack the side of the motorhome, gaps around both slide seals that let insects in at night and cold weather in any time, hydraulic fluid leaking out of the bedroom slide ram to pool under our bed, light fixtures that self-destruct driving down the road, insufficient caulking in the shower that caused a flood, a hot water heater that caused a mini-explosion of propane when it lit, a spring poking out of the sofa, oven gaskets that disintegrated the first time we opened the oven door, and a stove burner that would not turn off unless I went outside to shut off the propane, not to mention several minor irritations caused by lack of quality and finish, now the side of the motorhome is delaminating.

After repeated promises to do something, and failures to follow through, my comments in the *Gypsy Journal* (copies of which were sent to the president of Fleetwood) seem to be getting through to somebody. We were scheduled to bring the rig into the factory in mid-February for repairs. Fleetwood's representative originally said the motorhome would be in the shop four to six weeks, and they would pay for a motel for us during the period it was out of service. But by the time their confirmation letter arrived, the story had changed, and Fleetwood wrote they will reimburse us $45 per day for a room. Anyone know where you can get a room in southern California for that kind of money, that does *not* have mirrors on the ceiling and rent by the hour?

We hate being sidelined for so long a time, but if Fleetwood will really fix the problems this time, it's worth it. But since this

Meandering Down The Highway

will be our eighth trip into a repair facility in five months, we're not holding our breath. We remain terribly dissatisfied with this motorhome and would be delighted if Fleetwood would just give us our money back and let us go purchase a quality product, which our Pace Arrow Vision most certainly is not.

In a letter dated January 20, 1999, Tina Beck, Fleetwood's Service Administrator, wrote "It is our goal to constantly provide the highest quality products and services. At times, however, we are unable to achieve this goal, and we sincerely apologize. .....Though we can give you a thousand excuses for our mistake, it all boils down to one point - we were unable to meet your expectations. ....We would like to assure you that we are committed to resolving your concerns to your complete satisfaction." That all sounds good on the surface, but our experiences with Fleetwood have taught us words are cheap - almost as cheap as their products are made.

We arrived in Riverside mid-morning on February 15, and it was immediately obvious there were more frustrations in store for us. John, the Service Advisor assigned to our coach, came across to us as a young man with a chip on his shoulder. Almost the first words out of his mouth were that we were not getting all of the repairs done that we have complained about. He told us they would repair the cracked side of the motorhome, the carpeting damaged by the hydraulic leak, and the slideout seals. He informed us that the delamination was caused by customer negligence. As he explained it to us, *we* are responsible for sealing the seams in the side of the motorhome Fleetwood built. Ongoing problems with the stove, the oven gaskets, the sofa, etc. were not going to be repaired. Once I stood on my hind legs and bellowed, he finally agreed to repair the delamination on a one time basis, as a "customer accommodation." The rest of the problems are left up to us to find solutions to. This guy, with his

Meandering Down The Highway

rude attitude, was a perfect example of how *not* to treat unhappy customers. In other words, a perfect Fleetwood employee.

I know it may seem to some readers that we're on a vendetta against Fleetwood. I would urge anyone with a computer and Internet access to log into the RV Consumer Group Court of Public Opinion at www.RV.org. There are at least 17 complaints listed against Fleetwood, far more than any other manufacturer. That has to tell you something. We know we're stuck with our lemon, in fact, whenever we talk to a dealership about trading it in, they make it obvious they don't want to touch the darn thing. But if my words here will help another consumer avoid making the mistake we did in purchasing this nightmare, maybe something positive will come out of it.

So here we are, off the road for four to six weeks while our rig is in the shop. We'll be making several short trips to collect information for our next issue, and hopefully we'll be back on the road with at least some of our problems resolved. That first night out of our motorhome, we felt lost. Within a few days, hitch itch was really getting to us. We love our life on the road, and have so many adventures awaiting us just down the road and over the next hill. Until next issue, hope to see you in our travels.

Meandering Down The Highway

Meandering Down The Highway

May-June, 2000

So what's with these ridiculous fuel prices? I promised Miss Terry I'd give up editorializing when I quit the community newspaper business, but I just have to comment on the way the American public is getting shafted by the petroleum industry. Didn't we fight a war over in the Mid-East a few years ago to bring some semblance of stability to the region? Now our reward for the investment of American lives and military power is to have OPEC reduce production and drive prices into the stratosphere. Back in the old days, before we got so darned politically correct, we would have acted like the imperialists we were when we conquered this continent, and once we ran Iraq out of Kuwait, we would have seized the oilfields in both countries for ourselves. Now, before you go telling me that nice nations like ours don't do things like that, go have a chat with a Native American. Prices were so high the last time we were in California that some service stations were giving away a free motorhome with every tank full of gasoline purchased.

Radio Radicals

Driving through the night somewhere in Arizona, and a late night radio program is coming in from some paranoid type broadcasting from the middle of the Nevada desert. Everything seems to be a commie plot, some scheme to implement a New World Order, or a government coverup. The announcer keeps telling us that if we're not paranoid, we're not paying attention. Tonight's topic is cattle mutilations in Oregon, and a self-proclaimed "expert" is telling us that it's the work of space aliens.

Meandering Down The Highway

Call me naive, but I have to believe that if some being from another galaxy has the intelligence and technology to build a space craft, travel through the universe, and land on earth undetected, they'd have more on their agenda than giving a heifer a hysterectomy. But then again, what do I know? Until I started listening to late night radio, I never knew my dentist was implanting microchips in my fillings so Big Brother can keep track of me.

Off The Road and Homeless

If we ever had any second thoughts or nagging doubts about whether we made the right decision when we became fulltimers, being stuck off the road for some six weeks while our motorhome was in the factory removed them. Sure, it was fun having a big bathroom, with a huge shower and a real bathtub to soak in, and Miss Terry enjoyed playing chef in our friend's full size kitchen for a while. But those attractions wore thin real quick, and within just a week or so we had itchy feet and were getting bored. By the time the call finally came from Fleetwood that the work on our rig was completed, we were anxious to be back on the road. For us, the gypsy life of fulltime RVers is the only life we want to live. We owe our friend Mike Howard in Kingman, Arizona a big thank you for putting up with us for so long.

We spent most of the time our rig was in the factory in Kingman, Arizona, putting issue #5 together and getting it printed in Flagstaff. We also wandered over to Bullhead City and up to Henderson, Nevada during our homeless period. I always love seeing the gorgeous blue water of Lake Mead backing up to Hoover Dam. Most of Highway 93 between Kingman and the dam is now four lane divided highway, except for about twelve miles on the Arizona side of the dam, and a few miles on the Nevada side. There is always a crowd of people at the dam, and drivers have to be extra alert. Twice pedestrians busy sightseeing walked in front of us, making for a couple of frantic brake tests.

Meandering Down The Highway

Hoover Dam is quite an engineering marvel, and the electricity it provides supplies millions of people with power. Over the years, I've heard that at least one construction worker who was killed in the dam's construction still lies entombed inside its massive concrete walls. Turns out that's just another urban legend, just like the old story of the mangler who preys on neckers on Lovers Lane, or the fellow who buys a vintage Corvette for $25 because an errant husband ran off with his secretary and told his wife to sell his car and send him the money.

A couple of weeks later my friend Mike Howard and I drove back up to Henderson for the day. On the return trip, just as we dropped down into the canyon at Hoover Dam, Mike spotted a heard of mountain sheep lolling about just off the road a couple of hundred yards. One of Mike's life's goals has been to see mountain sheep live in the wild, but in all the years he's driven through the area, he had never seen one before. Now here were ten or twelve close at hand. Just one of the advantages of being a passenger instead of the driver, I suppose. There was a handy spot to pull off the highway, so we bailed out to get a better look at the critters. Now, I have to admit to committing a terrible professional sin here; I had two 35mm cameras in the truck, one equipped with a long range telephoto lens, but imagine my chagrin when I realized neither had any film in it! Here I am, a fellow who makes his living as a travel writer and photographer, and I was standing on the highway with a great photo opportunity without a roll of film to my name. Mike had a laugh or two at my expense over that foul up.

When we left Arizona March 19 to pick up our rig in Riverside, we ran into a nasty wind storm near Barstow, California. We stopped at a rest area for a few minutes, and about got the paint sandblasted off the side of our pickup. A few miles down the road a dust storm blew in, and it was pretty scary going for a couple of miles until the visibility improved.

Meandering Down The Highway

Somewhere on Interstate 40 a semi passed us with a sign on its trailer that read *"Be a flirt, pull up your shirt, it couldn't hurt."* Well, I'm here to tell you, that sign lied! When we rolled past that trucker and I honked the horn, he took one look at my rather large naked belly, dropped his CB microphone, and drove that Freightliner clear off the road and into the median. Spilled about three hundred VCRs and color TVs bound for a K-Mart in Modesto and a ton of assorted Tupperware products all over the highway! Not to mention, that seat belt chaffed the heck out of my left pectoral. So much for truth in signage.

We stopped in Lancaster, California and dropped off about 1,500 copies of the *Gypsy Journal* with the staff of the Spring Escapade for insertion into the welcome packets. When we walked into the Escapade office at the fairgrounds and I asked if it was a place a couple of homeless Escapees could get a hug, what a warm reception we received! Everyone dropped what they were doing and gave us that wonderful Escapee welcome we always get. Just being back with RVers for an hour or so made us feel more like our old selves, and showed us how much we had been missing. Ed and Gloria Helmuth had encouraged me to hold a class at the Escapade, my first attempt at public speaking, and I have to tell you, the butterflies were at work!

Not wanting to tackle the wind any longer, we checked into a Motel 6 in Lancaster for the night. There was a Carrow's Restaurant just across the parking lot, so we walked across for dinner. Big mistake. We've enjoyed the hospitality at several Carrow's restaurants across the country, and have always been pleased, but this one definitely needed a visit from the company inspectors. I ordered a soda, and when I told the waitress it was flat, she said yes, the machine was acting up. About twenty minutes later, while we still waited for our food, she finally came back and gave me a glass of tea. It was another twenty minutes or so before we finally got our meal, which left a lot to be desired,

Meandering Down The Highway

both in terms of quantity and quality. I could have chalked the entire experience up to just a bad night on their part, but the next morning I stopped in to get Miss Terry a cup of coffee to go, and they wanted to charge me ten cents for an extra dollop of cream. But what the heck, everything in life can't be rosy or it wouldn't be any fun, right?

I have to say here that we were pretty skeptical when we dropped our motorhome off at the Fleetwood factory in Riverside, especially given the attitude of the service writer who checked us in. But when we picked up our motorhome, almost all of the problems had been taken care of. Joey Mendoza, the service writer who delivered the coach to us really went out of his way to accommodate our needs. We arrived at the factory on a Monday afternoon, and there were several items that didn't meet our expectations. Joey apologized, put us up in a hotel overnight, and by 9 a.m. the next morning was on the telephone informing us that everything was completed. He even took care of a couple of last minute items that weren't on the original job list. Now, this is the kind of service Fleetwood needs to be providing all of the time to their customers. If the company honchos had any sense at all, they'd immediately promote Joey to Director of Customer Service. He went the extra mile and restored much of our lost faith in the company's customer service department. We still have an irritating thumping noise under the driver's floor, they didn't address the spring poking out of the sofa, and our rooftop satellite dish still doesn't work. But overall, we're a lot better off than we were when we dropped the motorhome off.

Tuesday, March 21, we were finally back in our motorhome and headed back to Arizona to pick up everything we had in storage while the rig was in for repairs. The wind had been terrible for two or three days, but our timing was just right, and by Tuesday it had dropped off. We picked up the rig and drove to Desert Hot Springs, where we spent the night at Western

Meandering Down The Highway

Horizons Desert Pools Resort.

We had just backed into our site when Charles and Viola Johnson, from Menasha, Wisconsin stopped by to order a subscription to the *Gypsy Journal*. They had received a sample copy in their membership packet from Passport America just a few days earlier, and were surprised to spot the signs on our truck, parked two spaces down from their rig. It's always fun to make new friends as we travel. One thing about the RV lifestyle, you'll only be lonely if you want to be. RVers are among the most friendly, outgoing people you'll find anywhere.

Do RVers have a preferred CB radio channel? I know lots of us monitor Channel 19, which is used by professional truckers, but I've seen hundreds of RV with antennas, and have seldom talked to another RVer on the CB radio while I was traveling. I know we all try to keep Channel 19 open for the working truckers out there, but I was wondering what channels RVers use, if any in particular?

I've Got A Greyhound Feeling

Lately we've become enamored with bus conversions. (Actually, *I've* become enamored with bus conversions. Miss Terry just grins and bears it, much like she did when I wanted to build a house out of straw bales, or when I wanted to drive the entire length of Route 66 in our old Corvette.) We had planned to attend the Bus Conversion Convention in Sacramento the week before Spring Escapade, but got a telephone call from *Bus Conversions* magazine telling us the convention had been postponed because California authorities have said they would issue citations to anyone driving a motorhome or bus conversion over 40 feet in length. It looks like the convention will be held either in Las Vegas or Laughlin, Nevada sometime in October.

Leave it to California bureaucrats to make life difficult any way they can. I've always said California was like a huge bowl of cereal - fruits and nuts surrounded by flakes. There are some

Meandering Down The Highway

really great places to visit in California, but their efforts to make life miserable for RVers are having a definite negative impact not only on the RVing community, but the economy of communities that depend on RVer dollars.

I've discovered a couple of good magazines for anyone interested in bus conversions. *Bus Conversions*, (3431 Cherry Avenue, Long Beach, California 90807) has been around for quite a few years, and has a lot of good information in it. A relative newcomer to the field, but very impressive indeed, is the bi-monthly *The Private Coach Enthusiast*, (P.O. Box 125, Dell Rapids, S.D. 57022). In addition to the magazine, the latter publishers also send out a monthly classified publication, *Private Coach Flyer*, with lots of buses listed for sale.

Now, anyone that knows me understands that I have absolutely no business being interested in converting a bus. Any task that requires me to pick up any tool more complicated than a Phillips screwdriver is cause to have an emergency medical response team standing by, and mechanics all across this great land of ours have put their children through college on the proceeds from undoing all of the projects I have undertaken. But a guy can dream, can't he? Just the thought of rolling down the highway in a big old bus, with all that chrome and stainless steel gleaming in the sunlight makes my heart skip a beat or two. But realistically, I know I'm not up to the chore of converting a bus, and even if I was, Miss Terry would balk at keeping those stainless steel slabs on the sides of the bus polished to perfection. The people we've talked to who have buses tell us you don't really *have* to be all that mechanical to own a bus, all you really have to do is stuff those big old storage bays underneath the bus full of $100 bills and you'll be just fine.

Our First Escapade

The Escapees Club Spring Escapade was April 16-21 at the Antelope Valley Fairgrounds in Lancaster, California. Since I

Meandering Down The Highway

was teaching a class, we arrived on Friday night, April 14. There were RVs lined up dry camping on the street next to the fairgrounds, and we spent Friday night parked with them. Saturday morning we moved onto the racetrack at the fairgrounds with other volunteers. Mike and Pam Steffen, whom we had met at the Life on Wheels Conference in Idaho last summer, were parked next to us, and we had the chance to renew acquaintances.

The Escapade was quite an experience. Over 1,300 RVs were on hand, swelling the population of Lancaster. Sunday night a heavy storm rolled through southern California, dumping over a quarter inch of rain on us in the next 30 hours or so. The dirt racetrack where so many of us were parked quickly became known as Mud Lake, and everybody found themselves wading in thick mud to get to their rigs. But just about everybody seemed to grin and bear it, and eventually the sky turned blue and the ground dried up.

I have to tell you, I was absolutely terrified at the thought of teaching a class at the Escapade. I just am not a public speaker, and the closer we got to the time for my class, the more nervous I became. In fact, my class was scheduled for 10:30 Monday morning. Miss Terry and I attended Joe Peterson's class first, which ran from 8:30 to 10 a.m., and I had to leave early to run back to our rig and throw up before I could face all those people from the other side of a microphone.

The amazing thing was that once I got up on the stage and got going, the class went fine and I had a great time. The hour went fast, and after it was over several of the people in the audience stopped by to tell me how much they enjoyed it. I must have done something right, because before I knew it, my name was on the list to teach classes at the Fall Escapade in Goshen, Indiana in September and again at Spring Escapade next year in Chico, California.

We met up with several friends we had crossed paths with

Meandering Down The Highway

earlier, including Phyllis and Ron Frey, Marcia Polk, Dennis and Pat Swann, and Henry and Linda Butler. It's always nice meeting up with old friends again, and one of the nicest things about the RVing lifestyle is the many people we run into again and again as we wander around the country.

We also had the chance to meet some of our readers and finally put faces with names on mailing labels. Sal and Bonnie Bellomo, and Tony and Karen Steflik were among the readers we finally got to meet face to face. Wherever we go, our RVing friends help us out by taking bundles of the *Gypsy Journal* to pass out at RV parks where they are going. This has really helped us increase our circulation, and new readers are coming in from every corner of the country. Bob and Peggy Herlocker were among the Escapees who offered to help spread the word, and it is much appreciated by Terry and myself. There were other friends at Escapade, both new and old, but space and my limited gray cells don't allow me to name everybody. That doesn't mean each and every one of them wasn't appreciated.

One of the things that really impressed me at Escapade was the Market Area, where vendors were selling all sorts of neat things for RVers, from auxiliary braking systems to water purifiers to cleaning supplies. I had quite a conversation with one of the seminar speakers who was talking about how fast communication technology is changing. We thought we were really up to date when we got a modem to connect our laptop computer to our digital phone for wireless e-mail access, which works about half the time. But now I learn that technology has made is possible to download information through a satellite dish, and the experts say that within a year or so we'll be able to have two-way Internet access through satellite dish technology. We may have conquered the frontiers of the continent a hundred years ago, but the frontiers of technology are being opened up further every day. To me, that's very exciting, and it will make life much

Meandering Down The Highway

easier for those of us on the road.

The Escapade ended on Friday morning, and we left the fairgrounds and drove over to Western Horizons Pyramid Lake Resort near Gorman on Interstate 5, a distance of about 50 miles. As we rolled west on Route 138, orange poppies were in bloom alongside the road, spreading out to the foothills. Terry's sharp eyes spotted a coyote foraging for ground squirrels or whatever else would fit on his dinner table.

Several of the Escapees from Lancaster came over to Pyramid Lake after the Escapade. We needed the time to unwind, and to catch up on laundry and housekeeping duties we had neglected during the Escapade. We had planned to spend four or five days at Pyramid Lake, but the Santa Ana winds were blowing at maximum force, and it was almost impossible to step outside without being blown sideways. By Easter Sunday we had cabin fever and were ready to take off, but decided to give it another day.

Easter afternoon and we're sitting inside our RV being rocked by wind gusts. Treetops are almost touching the ground in the gale force winds. Miss Terry looks outside and notices two rabbits playing in the middle of the RV park. Are these the guys who deliver the Easter eggs?

Moving On

One great thing about living in an RV - if you don't like the weather or the neighbors, you can just roll up the sewer hose and leave. We had planned to spend a few days at Pyramid Lake and use it as a base for a quick visit to my sister Maggie in Bakersfield, but by Monday morning the wind was still blowing with incredible strength. Listening to the CB radio, I heard that as soon as you got out of the Grapevine Pass, the wind was gone. We checked out of the RV park and hit the road for calmer surroundings.

Backtracking to Lancaster, we turned north to hook with

Meandering Down The Highway

Highway 58 and pointed the nose of the RV east. Just as we had heard on the radio, within a couple of miles of leaving the Grapevine behind us, the wind lessened dramatically, and what there was became that most elusive of RV phenomena, a tailwind. We scooted right along, picked up Interstate 15 at Barstow and began the long uphill climb toward Nevada.

 We stopped at Whiskey Pete's Casino at Primm, Nevada long enough to take a picture of the car outlaws Bonnie and Clyde were driving when they were killed in an ambush on a Louisiana back road back in the 1930s. Someone told me you're not supposed to take pictures in a casino, something about protecting the privacy of Sunday school teachers who might be there spending the collection money and philandering businessmen who told the wife they were at a sales conference in Oklahoma City. So don't tell anyone where the photo of the shot up old car came from, okay?

 We had originally planned to check into Destiny's Oasis Las Vegas RV Resort, but other Coast to Coast members had told us that it's impossible to get a spot at Coast to Coast's rate. Sure enough, when I called they said there were no Coast to Coast spots available. When I inquired about Passport America, the rate quoted was over $17 a night. Instead we took a spot across the street at the Silverton RV Resort and Casino. With our FMCA discount, it was less than Destiny Oasis, and from what I saw of the two facilities, just as nice.

 When we went inside the office to register, we met up with Doug and Dee Boswell, fellow Escapees we had met at the Escapade. Dee was feeling a bit under the weather and they were on their way back east to a medical appointment. Our friends got the site next to us, and Doug came over to help us coax a stubborn pin loose on our tow bar.

 Soon after we got set up, Don and Sue Townsend stopped by to introduce themselves. They had picked up a stack of the *Gypsy*

Meandering Down The Highway

Journals somewhere in Arizona and took them to a Newmar rally in Pahrump, Nevada to distribute. So many nice folks are out there helping us spread the word that it's no wonder our subscription list is growing so fast. The Townsend's had spotted our rig and came over to see the motorhome from hell first hand. We had a very nice visit with our new friends, and promised to look them up when we get back to New York, where they will be this summer.

I really want to like Las Vegas. There was a time when I used to visit Glitter Gulch pretty regularly, but these days the Las Vegas of old is long gone. It's too crowded, too plastic (not that it was ever anything else) and just too *much* for my tastes. We had thought we might spend a couple of days there, wander over to Fremont Street to see the laser light show, and maybe even pig out at a buffet or two. But just a little bit of driving around in all that traffic was enough to change our minds.

We had been craving a pizza, so I decided we'd go to the New York, New York Casino. Surely they had a good Italian restaurant where we could get a real New York style pizza. Bad idea. The casino is actually pretty interesting, with it's replica Statue of Liberty out front and the Big Apple decorating theme. One area is a recreated New York City neighborhood, complete with replica half-size apartment buildings, shops, delicatessens and restaurants. There are even manhole covers with steam coming out of them on the cobblestone streets. We had a good time strolling around taking in all the sights. If only the pizza had been as good as the motif. To say it was mediocre would have been an overstatement. I've had worse pizza, but it usually came out of a frozen food section and spent some time in a microwave. Looking around at the other diners, then back at our overpriced meal, the thought that never had so many paid so much for something so bad crossed my mind. Oh well, it's all part of the adventure.

Meandering Down The Highway

Some Days Are Diamonds, Some Days Are Stones

The next morning, before leaving the Silverton RV Resort, I stopped into the office to inquire about leaving some sample copies of the *Gypsy Journal* for other RVers. The two young girls at the counter were busily engaged in a contest to see who could sit on her chair the longest and avoid helping a customer, and it seemed to be a pretty even match, with two or three customers getting noncommital answers to questions as the young ladies discussed their love lives and giggled together about some juicy bit of gossip.

We headed out of Las Vegas and began a long, frustrating day. Things started off badly when we stopped at the Flying J for gasoline and propane. Most of the Flying J truck stops around the country have been very nice, and the company goes out of its way to make RVers welcome - with two exceptions, Kingman, Arizona and Las Vegas. The Kingman location is laid out in such a way that, if someone is parked in a regular vehicle in marked parking spaces in front of the restaurant, they can block a large RV from pulling out after fueling. We ran into that situation once, and had to wait while they paged the driver of a pickup truck and he left his meal to come out and move out of our way. The Las Vegas Flying J didn't have an RV fuel island, and it was too crowded in the automobile section for our big rig to get into. They also didn't have any propane. We'll scratch that one off our list of stops to return to.

We drove two miles down the highway and got off at a Pilot Travel Stop, where me managed to squeeze in next to a pump and get some gas. Like Flying J, they also didn't have propane. Getting out of the place was a bit of an adventure, as several impatient drivers cut across our nose to beat us to the exit, causing a couple of hard stomps on the brake pedal on my part.

Leaving Las Vegas, we spotted the Air Force's precision flying team, the Thunderbirds, flying in close formation near the

Meandering Down The Highway

highway. The Thunderbirds fly out of Nellis Air Force Base near Las Vegas, and are a common sight as they practice in the clear desert sky. We made good time across the rest of Nevada and crossed into the narrow strip of Arizona that makes absolutely no sense being a part of the rest of the state south of the Grand Canyon. The trip through the Virgin River Gorge was interesting, tall red rock walls reminiscent of Sedona, Arizona or maybe the Painted Desert towering over a twisting roadway that curved, climbed and dipped for about ten miles. In just over a half hour we were out of Arizona and crossed into Utah.

This was my first trip to the Beehive State, and now I can lay claim to having been in all of our 50 states. The Utah Welcome Center had a lot of good brochures, which we added to our collection. I wanted to ask the man working behind the counter a couple of questions, but a tourist from Israel was busy recounting her entire experience in traveling around the United States, including a minute by minute report on her itinerary, her opinion of every place she had been (none compared favorably to her home country), and the people she had met along the way (most of whom were incompetent, rude, pushy, and self-centered). Unable to slip a word in edge-wise, we finally gave up and left.

At St. George, we stopped at a grocery store to stock up, and while Miss Terry was shopping, I tried to track down a place to get propane, since we were almost out. The girl at the store where I asked for advice subscribed to the theory that if you are young enough, cute enough, and blonde enough, you don't have to be intelligent, polite, or helpful to strangers to your town. I found a phone book and called three different businesses listed in the yellow pages under Propane. One call was answered by a lady who told me "Mike does the propane, but he's not here today" before she hung up. The second place I called put me on hold and never came back, and the third business was out of propane and waiting for a truck to arrive. Meanwhile Terry was having a bad

Meandering Down The Highway

time in the Albertson's grocery store - she was taking an item off a shelf when she jabbed her arm on a broken shelf bracket, getting a nasty cut that bled pretty hard for a while before she was able to get a towel and stop it.

A call to Harrisburg Lakeside RV Resort, where we planned to spend a few days, brought us the advice that we should be able to get propane at the Texaco on Highway 9 near the resort. If the Texaco didn't have propane, we were assured that the Chevron a mile or so down the road would definitely have it.

We found the Texaco - no propane. Not even a tank. The Chevron (actually more like two or three miles down the road) did sell propane, but the way the parking lot was laid out, we needed to unhook our dinghy first, then I would have to pull into the parking lot and back up to the tank. No problem, we can handle that. The thermometer was hovering around 90 degrees, and we were hot, tired and thirsty. Add to that even more frustrated when I backed up to the propane tank, only to learn they were *out* of propane. We ended up leaving our pickup at the RV park, driving ten miles back to St. George, where we paid almost $2 a gallon, but finally got our propane tank filled.

We quickly found out that if you're driving a motorhome in St. George, Utah, you need about five sets of eyes. Drivers there seem to think nothing of cutting you off, pulling out in front of you, of changing lanes and leaving it up to the RVer to find someplace to go to avoid a collision. We arrived back at the RV park crabby, tired, and overheated. I told Terry that she needed to see everything in Utah she ever wanted to see in the next few days, because if our introduction to the state was any indication of what lay in store for us, I never planned on returning. We got onto our site, hooked up, and tried to mellow out after our long, hot, frustrating day. Crawling into bed, we hoped the next day would bring happier memories and better experiences for us in our visit to Utah.

Meandering Down The Highway

Utah Is Ugly

We're sitting in our space in Harrisburg Lakeside RV Resort, just outside Hurricane, Utah. Everybody seems to be grouchy in Utah. The scenery is spectacular, but we've been out and about all day long, and rudeness seems to be running at epidemic proportions. Is it just us, a carryover from the day before, or does everyone get the cold shoulder in southern Utah? The state has some of the most beautiful scenery in the world, but the overall impression we have so far is that the place *feels* ugly.

This RV park is located on the site of the former ghost town of Harrisburg, and the ruins of an old stone building stand at the entrance to the park. Harrisburg was founded by Moses Harris in 1862, three years after he helped settle San Bernardino, California. The community began on the shore of the Virgin River, but a flood forced the settlers to move further up Quail Creek to the Cottonwood Creek fork. Due to the many huge rocks in the area, the homes were built of stone, and rocks gathered while clearing the fields were used to establish property lines. Today several of these stone fences are still visible. By 1864 there were sixteen families living in Harrisburg, with a total of 128 people. The town's population peaked at 200 in 1868, with many of the residents employed by the nearby Silver Reef mine. The community didn't last long - by 1892 repeated flooding had driven most of the people away.

We've been in fifteen states since we started on the road, and stayed in everything from truck stop parking lots to luxury RV resorts, but this is the most unfriendly place we've ever been in. Last evening we went for a walk, and greeted three couples sitting at a picnic table. They stared at us like we were some strange life form, and wouldn't even wave back. Another couple passed us on their way to the pool, and looked the other way when we said hello. This place is depressing. Where are all of the happy campers we've met everywhere else we've been?

Meandering Down The Highway

The park charges $1.50 a day for cable television, even if you don't want it. We came in under our Coast to Coast membership, paying with a $6 camping card. Having to pay 25% extra for television really ticks me off. A fellow was checking in earlier today when I stopped in the store, and he really hit the roof. When he was told he didn't have any choice, he told the girl at the counter he never watched TV. She wouldn't budge, pay it or don't check in. He told his wife he intended to get every penny worth, and told her to leave every light on inside their rig all day long, and to keep the water running in the sink. Can't say as I blame him.

We spent part of the day touring St. George. The tour guide at the Joseph Smith Winter Home was the one of the few friendly people we've met here so far, but she spent as much time trying to convince us we needed to learn more about the Mormon church as she did telling us the history of the home and community. I did get a warm greeting at Settler's RV Park in St. George, where I stopped to drop off some sample copies of the newspaper. The fellow behind the counter was happy to get the papers, and said he would be sure everyone who came through the office got a copy. If we hadn't already paid for three days at Harrisburg Lakeside RV Resort, we would have moved to Settler's. Getting the Coast to Coast discount saves us a few bucks at the park we're in, but it would be worth the extra money to be around nice people. Tomorrow we're going to Zion National Park. Maybe we can find a smiling face there. *(Editor's note: We've heard since our visit to Harrisburg Lakeside Resort that the park has come under new ownership and things are much more pleasant.)*

Zion National Park

Forget every photograph you've ever seen of Zion National Park. They can't do it justice. Until you've actually stood at the base of those awesome sandstone cliffs or hiked the trails that wind below towering red rock formations, you can't comprehend

Meandering Down The Highway

the beauty of this place. Utah may be ugly, but Zion is more beautiful than I can find the words to describe it with.

We left the motorhome in the RV park and drove our pickup into Zion, which was a smart choice. There were plenty of RVs of every size, but finding a place to pull off the road to gawk (which you will do a lot of) would be nearly impossible in an RV of any size.

It was still early in the season, so the big crowds that invade the national parks later in the summer hadn't arrived yet. But there were still plenty of people scampering down the trails and staring in wonder at the beautiful sights in every direction. From the accents we heard, many of the visitors were from other countries.

Our first stop was the Visitors Center, where a small museum has some interesting exhibits on the geology of Zion and the forces of nature that created this unique, haunting landscape. The Visitor Center also has a short, free film that tells even more about Zion and what you can expect to experience on your visit. Following the movie, we joined about thirty other visitors for a short, informative talk on coyotes presented by one of the rangers. Coyotes are amazing animals, and while other species have retreated in the face of man's encroachment, they have expanded their turf until they are now found in every state except Hawaii. And the ranger said he's sure the crafty coyote is trying to figure out how to build a raft right now to make it to the islands.

Terry and I took the six mile long Zion Canyon Drive, then hiked the short half mile trail to Lower Emerald Pool, and met up with a Japanese woman coming back down the trail. The sight had moved her so much that it was obvious she was bursting to describe it to somebody, and we were the first people she encountered. "It's bootiful!" she told us with a wide grin and continued down the trail. This short hike is paved and accessible for wheelchairs, though it has a few steep inclines and will require

Meandering Down The Highway

assistance in places. At the pool, tree frogs serenaded us with a song that sounded exactly like the bleating of sheep.

I'm always amazed at how much detail my wife notices everywhere we travel. While it was all I could do to absorb the big picture of cliffs, blue sky, pine trees, and waterfalls, Terry also spotted and pointed out a squirrel, centipede, baby snake, lizards, dragon flies, birds, and frogs. You can read more about Zion National Park in a feature in this issue.

On Highway 9 a few miles east of the park's entrance is the town of Virgin, and the Virgin Trading Post, a typical tourist trap hawking rubber tomahawks for the kids, Southwestern trinkets, and such. But I had to take a couple of photos, and Terry ended up jabbing me in the ribs with her elbow when I remarked that maybe I should pick up a couple of virgins for sacrificial purposes. The two or three small towns between Interstate 15 and the park's entrance all seemed pleasant, and the people were friendlier than those we had met so far in Utah.

The Rocky Mountains

I had decided to make it my personal goal to strike up a conversation with at least one of our fellow campers, but after three days at Harrisburg Lakeside RV Resort even the most gregarious RVer has to admit he's in over his head and it's time to throw in the towel. I almost made it - on our last night we went for a stroll and said hello to a fellow walking his dog. Wonder of wonders, he responded with a hello of his own! But just like a neophyte hunter who gets buck fever and blows his shot at a trophy, I overreacted. "Beautiful evening, isn't it?" I asked. A look of confusion crossed his face, but I didn't catch it fast enough to stop myself. "What's your dog's name? He's a cute little fellow." He scooped his mutt up and retreated back inside his trailer. Oh well, I tried. I think the people around here have taken one dive too many in the same old gene pool and resent and/or are afraid of outsiders.

Meandering Down The Highway

We left early the next morning, heading north on Interstate 15. Guess what? Folks in Cedar City are a bit friendlier than their neighbors to the south in St. George. Gasoline is also cheaper, by about eight cents a gallon. We fueled up at a Conoco and even got a smile and "Have a safe trip" from the clerk.

As soon as we turned off of Interstate 15 and onto I-70, we started climbing uphill and fighting wind. The next few hours were a constant series of side winds, steep grades, and white knuckles. Our rig has never been easy to control on the highway under the best of circumstances, and the strong gusts of wind slamming into us had me fighting the steering wheel most of the way. We would have found a place to squat down and wait for the wind to die down, but the weather reports said a cold front was moving across the west and called for increasing winds over the next two days

This section of Utah is spectacular, with wind-sculpted red rocks, deep canyons, mesas, and vistas that will have you reaching for your camera at every turn. I was just too preoccupied with keeping the motorhome on the road to enjoy it as much as I could have. There are a couple of steep downhill runs, complete with runaway truck ramps. Shifting down to a lower gear, we took our time and negotiated them in good shape.

Crossing the state line into Colorado, we had planned to dry camp overnight at the Sam's Club or Wal-Mart in Grand Junction, but the parking lot at Sam's Club was small and cramped, and we couldn't find Wal-Mart, so we stopped for gas and continued on our way. It's probably just as well, I read later that much of Grand Junction was built on tailing piles from uranium mines. I doubt that we could have found a good night's sleep with all those people glowing in the dark.

About milepost 50, there is a tunnel on Interstate 70, and just before entering the tunnel is a sign that reads "Parking Area." We exited the highway and turned onto an old section of roadway that

Meandering Down The Highway

follows a bend of the Colorado River for a mile or so through a canyon and eventually returns to the Interstate. We found a wide spot and pulled over to boondock. We had the place all to ourselves, and after a walk down to the river to stretch our legs, we settled in. This is a good place to boondock, no more than five or six vehicles passed by in the entire time we were there, so it was pretty quiet. Our only neighbors were a few ducks swimming in the river. There was a fair amount of trash, evidence that kids probably use the place to party, but this Friday night we didn't have any company.

Interstate 70 through Colorado follows the course of the Colorado River for about 150 miles, and we watched the waterway change from a fairly placid river to rushing white water, where kayaks and rafts carried adventurers through thrilling rapids. We rolled through beautiful countryside dotted with occasional small towns and farms, and eventually reached the ski resort of Vail. Miss Terry's twin sons, Casey and Cody, live nearby and we had hoped to stop for a visit, but through a communications foul up our schedules didn't mesh and they were off at a bike race in Moab, Utah.

The climb through the Rocky Mountains is absolutely gorgeous, but I never want do it again in our present motorhome. Even with the addition of a Banks Power Pack, our rig just doesn't have the horsepower to make the pull. We struggled up through 10,600 foot Vail Pass, our speed droping down to about 20 miles per hour. By the time we reached the Eisenhower Tunnel, at over 11,000 feet, we were barely moving. The downhill slopes were almost as bad as I tried not to overheat our brakes or transmission as I used both to keep our speed down in the safe range. Strong wind gusts didn't do anything to help, either. I sure was jealous of those big diesel motorhomes that rolled past us uphill with power to spare, and cruised comfortably downhill with the aid of their

Meandering Down The Highway

engine brakes. If you have to drive a gasoline powered motorhome over the Rockies, I'd suggest unhooking your toad to make the trip easier. If we make the same trip again, I know we will. I understand the westbound trip through the mountains on I-70 is even harder.

Even at the end of April, there was still plenty of snow on the mountains and piled up alongside the highway. Truckers on the CB radio had been talking about a small herd of bighorn sheep alongside the highway on the westbound side, and we managed to spot them as we went past in the opposite direction.

We stopped at Lookout Mountain, on the eastern edge of the slope, to visit Buffalo Bill's Grave. The park where the old buffalo hunter is buried offers grand views of Denver and the prairie to the east, but the view was somewhat dimmed by haze this day. We stayed for a bit to pay our respects, then continued on downhill and stopped at Camping World just outside Denver to drop off a couple of bundles of sample newspapers.

Very Bad Weather

Leaving Denver on Interstate 25, we immediately ran into bad weather. Very bad weather. The cold front that had been moving west caught up with us, bringing dangerous wind, rain, and hail. Somewhere between Denver and Fort Collins we pulled into a truck stop to wait out the storm, and discovered every school kid in Wyoming and Colorado was there ahead of us. Apparently there was some sort of regional athletic championship going on somewhere nearby, and school buses from all over Wyoming and Colorado were pulled up so the young athletes could hit a couple of fast food restaurants while the drivers waited for the storm to pass.

We spent about an hour at a Wendy's, dawdling over hamburgers and watching the sky clear, then followed the school buses back onto the highway. Soon we began to see white alongside the highway, but it wasn't snow, it was hail. The storm

Meandering Down The Highway

had dumped hail up to two inches in diameter throughout the area. Knowing the damage that hail can do to RVs and vehicles, we were glad we had waited for the worst of the storm to pass.

The rain and hail may have preceeded us, but we still had wind to contend with, and it grew stronger as we headed north toward Wyoming. By the time we reached Cheyenne, it was getting impossible to hold the motorhome on the road, and the radio was reporting wind gusts up to 70 miles per hour in places. We pulled into the Flying J at Cheyenne and gassed up, at $1.29 a gallon with our RV Discount Club card. We were only wearing tee-shirts, but warmer clothing soon came out when we hit that cold air. The combination of temperature and wind chill put it at nine degrees, and the wind was still growing stronger.

One of the best things about traveling in an RV is that you don't *have* to deal with things like that. We had overnighted in this particular Flying J almost a year ago, and we knew there was a big parking area on the opposite side of the truck stop, away from where the truckers park. We pulled in among several other RVs and buckled down for the night.

All night long the wind slammed into the side of the motorhome, to the point where about 3 a.m. I though we might get knocked over. But come daylight we were still sitting on our wheels, and the storm had moved eastward across the plains. We were only about 80 miles from our destination in Torrington, Wyoming, where we planned to visit Terry's son Shawn and daughter Kelly and their families. The wind wasn't as severe as the night before, but it still made for slow going down Highway 85. We passed two small herds of antelope who seemed to have the right idea, they were hunkered down on the lee side of small hills watching all those oddball human creatures try to fight the wind in their noisy automobiles and recreational vehicles. What do you mean, dumb animals?

Kelly, a beautiful blonde who contradicts all those dumb

Meandering Down The Highway

blonde jokes we've heard, will be graduating from nursing school in a few days, so we've taken up temporary residence at a space in the Goshen County Fairgrounds, where we get full hookups for $8 a day while we await the big event. Gasoline prices are unbelievably low here, considering what we've been paying across the country. One gas station in Torrington was advertising gasoline for $1.26 a gallon, a full fifty cents a gallon less than we paid in Lancaster, California just a week ago! And this out in the middle of nowhere where the fuel has to be trucked in. Would someone explain that to me please?

Our supply of reading material was exhausted, so we drove to Scotts Bluff, Nebraska to hit a couple of used bookstores. On the return trip, we spotted several emus in a farmer's field just outside Morrill and stopped to get a better look at these strange looking giant birds. I've never seen an emu close up, and the six foot tall buzzard apparently wasn't too thrilled with his first look at an RVer either. As I started to shoot pictures, it squatted down and spread its wings out, then began to rock sideways, apparently in an attempt to make itself look more fearsome (like an emu isn't a fearsome sight already). When this failed to scare me away, the emu stood up and began to swell its throat to almost three times its normal size, and let out an awful noise that was a cross between a honk and a growl. I took a look at its talons, its height, and the thin fence between us and decided a guy really only needs a couple of pictures of an emu anyway and retreated back to the pickup.

You know you're in Wyoming when the local Chevrolet dealer has more pickup trucks for sale on his lot than he does cars. We'll spend a week or so here visiting grandkids and getting this issue of the *Gypsy Journal* out. We originally had hoped to have every issue of the newspaper printed and in the mail no later than the first week of the two month period it's dated. Obviously we

Meandering Down The Highway

were not able to make that deadline this time around. Being off the road for so long while our rig was in the factory put a real crimp in our style. But we've found that our original deadline was unrealistic as we travel around the country. Finding a newspaper printing plant capable of handling the job isn't hard to do, but getting them to work us into their established printing schedules can be difficult at times. Since we are a one time job, they shove us to the bottom of the list and print their regular customers first, which is understandable. So we need to revise our original deadline, much to our chagrin. We will still try very hard to get your *Gypsy Journal* to you in the first week of the publication period, but sometimes it may be a little later as we wait for a press time. I can guarantee you will always get your paper in a timely manner, but if it's a few days late, please understand that we are just as frustrated as you are, sitting somewhere waiting for those printing presses to start spitting out newspapers. We appreciate your patience.

From here we're off in search of new adventures somewhere down the road. We'll probably head toward the Midwest, but our travel plans are vague, which is just the way we like to keep them. Wherever we end up, we know there will be interesting people to meet and fun places to explore and write about for next issue. Until then, hope to see you in our travels.

Meandering Down The Highway

Meandering Down The Highway

July-August, 2000

Getting To Know Colorado

Snow in the middle of May? It's hard to believe, but that's what we encountered when we arrived in Cheyenne, Wyoming as we traveled south. We had battled strong headwinds from Torrington to Cheyenne, and pulled into the Flying J to refuel both our motorhome and ourselves. After we had finished our lunch, we came outside to be greeted by thick snowflakes. That's all the motivation I needed to point the nose of our rig for southern climes.

We arrived in Denver, Colorado right at 5 p.m., just in time for rush hour traffic. There were a few miles of stop and go on the south side of town, but overall it was a smooth trip, and we noticed that most of our fellow drivers were very courteous, giving us plenty of room to change lanes when we needed to.

About fifty miles south of Denver we pulled into Colorado Heights Camping Resort in Monument, which turned out to be one of the friendliest RV parks we've ever visited. We had called ahead to reserve a spot, and the office was closed when we arrived. Before we even found a spot to park and get hooked up, night managers Paulette and George pulled up in a golf cart to welcome us to the resort. It was a Thursday evening, and we had planned to spend a night or two at most, but the reception was so warm that we immediately changed our mind and decided to stay through the weekend. Actually, we didn't have much choice - that Sunday was Mother's Day, and Paulette insisted we stay and be

Meandering Down The Highway

their guests at the special dinner the resort was having for the moms in the park.

Colorado Heights is a beautiful park, complete with a well stocked fishing pond. I didn't get a chance to wet a line, but I did enjoy watching a grandfather introduce his young grandkids to the sport of fishing. One young fellow, maybe four years old, was thrilled to catch his first fish, an impressive rainbow trout. Grandpa thought the little fellow might not take too well to the fish cleaning process, so grandma took the youngster off while he filleted the catch. The next day I ran into them again, and asked the lad how his fish tasted. "Yummy," the little man said enthusiastically. "Grandpa cut their bodies off!" We spent four days at the resort while we explored the area around Colorado Springs, and everyone from the staff to our fellow campers was very friendly. This is one place we'll be going back to.

I was interested in visiting the United States Air Force Academy in Colorado Springs, so one windy afternoon we stopped by. Now, I have to be up front and tell you before we proceed that I am a snob. At least Miss Terry says I am, and who would know better than her? Back about a hundred years ago when I was young and had hair, I spent a couple of years at the United States Military Academy at West Point, New York. It was right at the tail end of the Vietnam War, and I guess the Army needed some place to keep me until my enlistment ran out, so I found myself trying to help teach cadets which end of a rifle went bang. I guess I'm prejudiced, but West Point has a sense of history and tradition to it. Those great granite walls at West Point have been witness to so much of our past. The institution has been serving our country since Revolutionary War days, and to walk in the footsteps of our great military leaders is quite an experience. During the course of my assignment to West Point, I paid a couple of visits to the Navy's top school at Annapolis, Maryland, and that place too has real history attached to it.

Meandering Down The Highway

The Air Force Academy, on the other hand, is a modern compilation of glass and steel that could just as easily be any college campus, if you took away the uniforms and the aircraft on display around the grounds. I guess that's understandable, since the Air Force itself is a relatively new branch of the service, coming into its own only after the close of World War II. Not that it doesn't play a critical role in training our nation's future military leaders, but the place just feels so *modern*. Even though we hope our country will never again call young men and women to face an enemy force, history tells us it will indeed happen one of these days. Having well trained leaders can help those young service members prevail and come home safe and sound. Charged with that task, the Air Force Academy meets its responsibilities well. I just miss the feel of stone and tradition around me.

Another day trip in Colorado Springs took us to the Pro Rodeo Hall of Fame. If you want to see more saddles, boots, Stetson hats, and gold and silver spurs in one place than you ever thought possible, this is a must see. The museum recognizes the great rodeo performers past and present, as well as the stock contractors, clowns, and others who make the sport of rodeo successful.

Albuquerque Adventures

We had a good time in the Monument/Colorado Springs area, but we needed to get on down the road, so after four nights at Colorado Heights, we hit the road again. South of Colorado Springs, we came across several convoys of soldiers rolling south in HumVees, trucks and buses. I commented to Miss Terry that the troops sure looked young, then remembered that I was only a teenager back when I wore the uniform too. My old Dad used to always say that we send young men to fight our wars because once they get a little older and wiser they wouldn't go. Funny, but as I get older I realize more and more just how smart my old man

Meandering Down The Highway

was. I wish he was still around so I could tell him so.

The terrible forest fire that destroyed so much of Los Alamos, New Mexico was still raging as we drove down Interstate 25, and though we were quite a distance away, the huge clouds of smoke told the sad tale. All over northern New Mexico the air was hazy with smoke. We encountered our own forest fire just outside of Pecos, several acres ablaze right alongside the highway. A helicopter was dropping buckets of water on the flames and fire trucks were parked in the right lane pouring more water to keep the fire under control. We had to sympathize with the fire fighters, working so hard in their heavy protective rubber clothing.

The wind was slamming us again, so we slipped into Hidden Valley Resort in Tijeras, just a few miles east of downtown Albuquerque. We had only planned to stay a night or two, but it wasn't until the morning of the fourth day that the wind had abated enough to allow us back on the highway. We took advantage of the time to get to know Albuquerque a little better.

We had visited Albuquerque before, and one place Miss Terry had been looking forward to getting back to was Bea's New Mexican Restaurant, a small eatery on Central Avenue. Bea's may not look impressive at first glance, just a tiny little place with vinyl booths, a causal staff, and a small parking lot. But that authentic down-home ambience is only a precursor to some of the best authentic Mexican food you'll find anywhere in the country. My navigator and soul mate is a bit of a snob herself, when it comes to food. The lady is an expert cook herself, and knows much more about what's good and bad than my rather pedestrian palate will ever be able to tell me. So when I tell you that no trip to Albuquerque is complete without a trip to Bea's, you know the place must be good. We had one of our favorite dishes, Carne Adovada, a spicy concoction of pork, chile and spices. Try it once and I guarantee you'll be a regular at Bea's just like us. But don't

Meandering Down The Highway

bring your RV, there is no place to park anything more than a car or pickup nearby.

Old Town Albuquerque is a can't miss place. The original settlement of Albuquerque, it's a maze of old adobe buildings housing interesting shops, restaurants, and art galleries, and Native American artists selling their silver and turquoise jewelry under the shade of awnings and porticos. We've visited Old Town several times, and always love it.

This trip we discovered the American International Rattlesnake Museum, where you can see enough venomous reptiles to feed your nightmares for at least a year or two. I'll never be a herpetologist, but I am getting better. I didn't reach for a gun once as we looked at diamondback rattlers, timber rattlers, sidewinders, and every other kind of buzzing, biting rattlesnake there is. As long as they stayed on their side of the glass and I stayed on my side, we got along just fine, thank you. The museum was very interesting, and I came away with quite a bit of new knowledge about rattlesnakes, I'll have to admit. Does this mean I now *like* the vipers? Not on your life. But I've mellowed out over the years and adopted a live and let live policy. Truth is, unmolested, rattlesnakes will go about their business and not bother anyone, and we humans should do the same.

All of nature depends on an elaborate system of checks and balances, and the same applies to the Rattlesnake Museum. Since I had to look at snakes, which I have a terrible fear of, Mother Nature balanced the scales by letting me meet a beautiful woman. The Reverend Diana Eksund was working the counter at the museum when we stopped in to visit, and she was just as friendly as she was pretty. When she's not collecting admissions at the museum and selling souvenirs, Diana is busy performing wedding ceremonies at the Chapel of Old Town. Lovely women introducing you to rattlesnakes, that's about as odd a combination as myself narrating a workout video, don't you think?

Meandering Down The Highway

We've made many wonderful new friends on the road, and two of the nicest are Rick and Laurie Phillips, fulltimers who we met last winter at Rainbow's End Escapees park in Livingston, Texas. We have been keeping in contact ever since by e-mail, and were thrilled to get a message that Rick and Laurie were also in Albuquerque. A couple of missed phone calls later, we had finally connected and made plans to meet for lunch the next day. The reunion was a great treat for all of us, and we had a nice lunch at Red Lobster and spent hours comparing notes on our travels since we had last been together. When it was time to part company again, we did so with hugs and promises to meet up again somewhere down the road.

Into The Oven

Try as we might, unfinished business seems to keep dragging us back to Arizona when we'd really much rather be somewhere else. I had an appointment in Tucson May 24, so we took Interstate 40 into Flagstaff, turned south to Camp Verde, where we spent a few days at Western Horizons Verde River Resort trying to work up the courage to face the extreme temperatures further south in the desert.

We put it off as long as possible, then finally drove down to Mesa, where Miss Terry's parents had arranged a parking place for us next to them at Carriage Manor Resort. From there, we would take care of our business and try to stay out of the 110 degree heat as much as possible. No matter how good your RV's air conditioners are, when it's that hot, life is uncomfortable at best. Though we were delighted to spend time with Terry's parents, Pete and Bess Weber, we would have preferred to visit them next to a cool stream in the Northwest if we could have.

The heat in the Arizona desert in the summertime isn't just higher temperatures. It's almost a living entity of its own, a malevolent force that sucks the very life out of you and leaves you drained and empty. Though I've had to live in the desert, no

Meandering Down The Highway

matter how much air conditioning there was, I've never been able to tolerate it. Many years ago I suffered an episode of heat stroke, and it seems that ever since, my body just cannot tolerate temperatures like this for more than a few minutes before I begin to feel the effects.

It's pretty amazing when you think of it - just a couple of weeks ago we saw snow in Wyoming, and last night the weatherman in Phoenix was predicting 113 degree heat for early next week. As soon as possible, we'll be heading for somewhere in the middle of the two extremes.

A Tucson Stop

We spent the Memorial Day holiday parked next to Terry's parents at Carriage Manor, and left Mesa on Tuesday, May 30. This was an easy travel day, a little over two hours to Tucson, where we stopped for a couple of days to visit family and friends.

On a visit to Tucson last year, we had stayed at Prince of Tucson RV Park and came away unimpressed. The park is attractive and has some amenities, but they seemed to want every nickel they could get out of us. When we asked if we could leave our rig in the park for about two hours after checkout time, parked off to the side and not hooked up to services, they wanted to charge us what we felt was an outrageous fee, especially since it was the off season and most of the park was empty. This trip we stayed at Tra-Tel RV Park, almost next door. The park is smaller and may not be as beautifully landscaped, but the people were much friendlier and the price definitely more reasonable. We had planned to stay under our Passport America membership at half off their regular rate, but the manager spotted our Escapees Club decal on our motorhome and gave us an even better discount. You've got to appreciate any place that goes out of their way to save you money.

After freshening up a bit from our drive, we drove across town to spend the evening visiting with my attorney, Roberta

Meandering Down The Highway

Jensen, who is a dear friend that goes a long way back. This was Terry's first chance to meet Roberta, and the ladies hit it off very well.

I lived in Tucson for many years, but the Old Pueblo has changed a lot in the decade plus I've been gone, and it was interesting to drive around town a bit and see what remains and what has changed. One thing that struck me as different, though I'm sure I just never noticed it before, is how dark Tucson streets are at night. There is very little in the way of street lighting, possibly due to efforts to reduce light pollution for nearby Kitt Peak Observatory.

We got back to Tra-Tel about 9:30 p.m., and the place was alive with jackrabbits! Miss Terry spotted a couple as we were pulling in, then a couple more, then suddenly the place was hopping (sorry, I had to use that line) with them. One furry little fellow ran right in front of the pickup, and I slowed down to avoid hitting him. He jumped so high he cleared the top of our hood, then went on his way!

Rabbits weren't the only critters keeping us company at Tra-Tel. The next morning I stepped outside and a covey of quail ran out from under the rig and scooted across the gravel parking lot to take shelter in quieter quarters under a fifth wheel parked nearby.

Even in the last week of May it was hot in Tucson. In fact it was so hot and dry I woke up one morning to a commotion outside the rig and peeked out the window to see two trees fighting over a dog. That was enough for us, and we hit the road.

Land Of Enchantment

New Mexico is called the Land of Enchantment, and I can see why. There is so much to see and do that one could spend a year within her borders and never cover it all. From desert to mountain top, New Mexico has history, scenic beauty and man-made attractions in enough variety to satisfy every taste.

The wind had followed us east from southern Arizona across

Meandering Down The Highway

the border, and by the time we hit Deming it was getting hard to handle the rig. Though it was only mid-afternoon, we pulled into the Escapees Club Dreamcatcher RV Park, our regular stop when we're overnighting in Deming. It proved to be a good move, since we had hardly gotten hooked up before a nasty sandstorm rolled in, rocking the motorhome on its jacks and reducing visibility to just a few yards. The storm didn't last long, though the high winds continued to blow most of the night.

It was over 100 degrees in Deming, and the RV park was pretty empty. Just a few rigs that had pulled in to get out of the wind. Early the next morning everybody hit the road again, us included. At Las Cruces, we turned northeast on U.S. 70 and began the long climb up toward Alamagordo. The road is a good four lane and the uphill slope is long, but fairly gentle. We hadn't gone far when I spotted a historic marker and had to pull off at the site where Lincoln County sheriff Pat Garrett was murdered in 1908. Mystery still surrounds the death of Garrett, who killed outlaw Billy the Kid in 1881. There is a dirt pullout at the sign, but we missed it and parked in the parking lot of a church next to the highway. That turned out to be fortunate, since the parking area around the sign was littered with nails and other sharp trash that would tear up a set of tires in no time. As it was, we got our shoes full of sand spurs and cactus bits walking over to read the marker.

Continuing up the hill, we passed through the little community of Organ. I kept a sharp eye out, but didn't spot one liver or kidney in the entire place. At the 5,719 foot summit of San Augustin Pass there is a wide rest area guarded by a missile, the first of many space projectiles we were to see in the next 24 hours. On a clear day the view of the Rio Grande Valley from the rest area is up to 70 miles, and it is well worth taking the time to pull over for. The rugged Organ Mountains are part of an ancient volcano and gave up a lot of gold, silver, copper and other metals during the mining period in this region. The rest area is fairly

Meandering Down The Highway

long, and we parked at the near end after pulling off the highway. While Miss Terry was using the bathroom in our RV, I stepped outside and decided to walk down to the other end of the rest area and take a few photos. I looked up to see our rig coming toward me, and my first thought was "I hope Terry's not still in the bathroom!" Fortunately she was behind the wheel, and just trying to save me the long walk back uphill.

Dropping down off the pass, we came to a turnoff for the White Sands Missile Range and took the short drive up to the Army base to see what there was to discover. Driving in, the highway had several ominous warning signs telling us that unauthorized photography was prohibited, no weapons were allowed, and that there was a danger of unexploded bombs laying around. I tucked my Nikon away with my machine gun and told Miss Terry to watch her step.

In spite of all the written warnings of doom, the guard at the Reception Center was very friendly, and after showing him our vehicle registration, proof of insurance, valid driver's license, marriage license, and rabies vaccination certificate, he issued us a pass that allowed us to drive about forty yards to the Missile Park and Museum, with its impressive outside display of rockets and missiles. We saw everything from Patriot missiles like those that helped us win Desert Storm to some of the early rockets that helped man venture into outer space. The museum's indoor exhibits included displays on an early day battle between the cavalry and Apaches led by the war chief Victorio that took place nearby, to the Trinity Site, where the first atomic bomb was detonated, to World War II. The museum is rather small, but it was well worth the couple of hours we invested to see it. The Missile Park displays some sixty rockets and missiles tested at White Sands. White Sands Missile Range encompasses 3,200 square miles, in which over 100,000 prehistoric sites are

Meandering Down The Highway

estimated to exist. 3,500 of these sites have been recorded and protected. Admission to the base and museum are free.

Back on the highway, we soon came to a U.S. Border Patrol checkpoint, where we assured the young inspectors that we were indeed U.S. citizens, not carrying any contraband or illegal aliens, and voted Republican.

Just across from the checkpoint is the entrance to White Sands National Monument, where we stopped to take in the small museum, which offers a free seventeen minute video about the monument, and gift shop, then drove the eight mile loop through part of the monument. If you've never been to White Sands, this is one trip you need to make. The sand is actually gypsum crystals, and looks just like snow as it piles up and drifts across the roadway. The ranger on duty told me they have to run a snowplow down the road twice weekly to keep the path open. Having lived in snow country for many years, I found myself automatically slowing down on the curves and trying to avoid skidding, even though it was over 100 degrees outside and the road was as dry as a good martini. Miss Terry commented that in spite of the heavy overcast to the west, the glare coming off the sand made her eyes hurt, and sunglasses definitely are required equipment when visiting. With miles of drifting sand, sculpted by the wind, and just a few plants sticking up here and there, it almost resembled a moonscape.

We spent the night dry camping at the Otero County Fairgrounds in Alamogordo. The fairgrounds has a large, paved parking lot, dump station, and a water spigot to fill your tanks, and it's all free. The temperature was fifteen degrees cooler than in Deming, and a storm had preceded us through the area, really cooling things off. For the first time in over a week, we enjoyed sleeping with our windows open and the air conditioning turned off.

Friday morning bright and early we were up and off,

Meandering Down The Highway

stopping at the National Space Hall of Fame (located appropriately enough on 2001 Drive), where we saw even more rockets, satellites, and space paraphernalia. The museum was interesting, and we learned a lot, but one thing really bummed me out. Tucked away under the flagpoles outside the place, away from all the fancy exhibits and displays, is a simple plaque marking the grave of Ham, the first chimpanzee blasted into outer space. I kind of felt sorry for the little fellow. I mean, think about it, he was just minding his business back home in Africa and some clown kidnaps him, stuffs him in a spacesuit, straps him into the nosecone of a rocket and lights a wick somewhere, and the next thing he knows he's dodging asteroids and listening to William Shatner droning on about final frontiers. After all that, do we set him up in a nice little two bedroom bungalow somewhere with a cute little girl chimp and give him a minivan and a pension? Nope, they shunted him off to a zoo to live out his days, then buried him under a flagpole! Where's the justice in that, I ask you?

Leaving Alamogordo on Highway 70, we traveled east, climbing up through the Mescalero Apache Reservation to Ruidoso, home of some of the biggest purses in horse racing. On the Reservation, we saw several modern mobile homes and houses with a traditional teepee in the yard. Other homes seemed to forgo the teepee in favor of a satellite dish. The times, they are a'changing. At the top of the climb, Apache Summit, it is 7,190 feet. Starting downhill, the ancient volcano Sierra Blanca, towering 12,003 feet over the Tularosa Basin, greets you. The country is beautiful, heavily treed with Ponderosa pines, reminding us of our home town back in Show Low, Arizona.

Several dry winters in a row have had their impact, and as we came into town signs everywhere were warning against open fires, barbecue grills, smoking outdoors or anything else that might cause a forest fire. Having lived in the middle of forest

Meandering Down The Highway

country, we could empathize with the concerns local folks had. One careless camper or thoughtless smoker could set the entire tinderbox on fire and wipe out a whole community. In New Mexico that duty is reserved for the U.S. Forest Service.

We crossed the Lincoln County line, into the land of Pat Garrett and Billy the Kid, where every roadside souvenir shack, hamburger stand, and tourist trap seems to bear the name of the infamous gunslinger. There seemed to be a multitude of places selling chainsaw carvings and statues alongside the highway in Ruidoso.

East of Ruidoso, the road took us through high desert, with a verdant little valley paralleling the route for miles, lush with trees and grass. There were quite a few small RV parks along the highway, at least one offering fishing in its own trout lake. We also passed Fox Cave, protected by cyclone fencing, with a huge billboard announcing it was the hideout of, who else, Billy the Kid. The route is part of the Billy the Kid Scenic Byway, which carries travelers on a big loop through that portion of New Mexico the bandit hung out in during the bad old days. Just outside of San Patricio we spotted an old shack on the left with a sign reading "Handmade Quilts" and several beautiful examples of the quilters' art hanging outside. A historical marker near San Patricio told of the area's involvement in the Lincoln County War, including the raid by a posse in July, 1878, searching for Billy the Kid and his gang of cutthroats, known as the "Regulators."

Approaching Roswell, signs told us about UFO gift shops, UFO-theme restaurants, even a radio station advertising UFO Country. One shop had a sign offering Southwestern and UFO gifts. What would that be, Kachina dolls wearing space suits? I have a theory. If a UFO actually did crash in Roswell back in the 1950s, killing all aboard, I think it was actually a mass suicide when they realized they traveled through a couple of dozen

Meandering Down The Highway

galaxies to get here, and ended up in Roswell. The place is ugly and boring. We didn't see any aliens, though I did spot two space cadets sharing a bottle outside a convenience store.

We passed through Roswell about noon on a Saturday and the place was almost deserted. Either everyone was sleeping off their Friday night partying, or maybe they had been beamed up to a place where there is intelligent life. Gasoline was thirteen cents a gallon more in Roswell than it was back down the road in Alamogordo. There were several RV parks in Roswell, ranging from an empty corner of someone's back yard to nice looking parks with full hookups. All in all, Roswell didn't impress us.

One thing that struck me as odd was that we passed several little used car lots on the way into town, and every one of them had a Corvette for sale. Many more Corvettes than you would expect to see for sale in a town the size of Roswell. I guess when you've got a UFO chasing you, you need a fast car to make your getaway.

Music Stars, Free Campgrounds, And The World's Tallest Windmill

From Roswell we took U.S. 380 toward Texas. Nearing the state line at Tatum, we stopped to check out the free RV campground in the city park. It was too early to stop for the day, but the place looked good and we filed it away for future reference. We crossed into Texas, and stopped at Brownfield to fill our gas tank. Our mileage has been improving with every tank recently, even though we had been running our dash air conditioning and the generator to use the roof AC back in the desert. I figure if things keep going like this, we could hit 25 miles per gallon by the end of the summer, and I might actually start to *like* this rig of ours. Brownfield is a typical small Texas town, with one exception - the streets of the old downtown area are all brick, taking you back in time a generation or so.

There had been thunderstorms all through the area, and the humidity was way up, but it was still much more comfortable than

Meandering Down The Highway

it was back in the desert. We had planned to stop at one of two free city RV parks from our list, either in Levelland or Littlefield, both on Highway 385. We came to Levelland first, a nice clean little town of modest homes and well tended yards. We pulled in to check out the RV park. Six or seven full hookup sites, shade trees and well trimmed grass. Since it was still early, we decided to continue on another thirty miles or so to Littlefield and the Waylon Jennings Free RV Park. Looking back, I think the park in Levelland was probably a bit nicer, though both were adequate.

Littlefield named its park for favorite son country music star Waylon Jennings. The park has water, electric and a dump station. We arrived on a Saturday evening, and a Mexican church was holding a tent revival in the park. We couldn't understand the singing, but the music was good and we found ourselves tapping our feet throughout the evening. Littlefield's downtown area seemed to have almost as many empty storefronts as occupied ones. I was expecting to find a museum or something about Waylon Jennings' life, but aside from a sign in the RV park saying he was born here, there doesn't seem to be any real interest locally.

Sunday morning we left the rig in Littlefield and drove the 35 miles or so into Lubbock to visit the Buddy Holly Memorial. Lubbock was the home of several music stars, including rock and roll pioneer Holly, Otis Redding, Mac Davis, and Tanya Tucker, who was born in Lubbock before moving on to Arizona. The Buddy Holly Center was closed, but we did manage to see his statue, and found his grave in the town cemetery. Fans from around the world come to Lubbock to pay their respects at Holly's grave, and traditionally leave a guitar pick to insure the music never dies. While I was standing on a street corner in Lubbock taking pictures, a car carrying Tom and Jacki Stewart, tourists from England, stopped to ask directions. Their goal is to visit each of the fifty states, and they were on their third or fourth two-week

Meandering Down The Highway

visit to the United States covering as much ground as they could. We chatted a bit, gave them a copy of the *Gypsy Journal*, and went our separate ways. Several weeks later I got an e-mail from them telling me they had arrived back in Jolly Olde England safe and sound, but that the airlines had lost their luggage. That never happens when you travel in an RV.

Back at our RV in Littlefield, I was checking out my Texas road map and found a notation that Littlefield is the site of the world's tallest windmill. Imagine that, the World's Tallest Windmill, and we were right there! We piled back into the truck and went off in search of this amazing architectural wonder. After a slightly miscalculated start, Miss Terry's eagle eye spotted the windmill right on the edge of downtown. Turns out this is only a replica of the original World's Tallest Windmill! The original World's Tallest Windmill was erected in 1887 on the three million plus acre XIT Ranch nearby. The 132 foot windmill was located in a canyon, and had to be so tall to catch the wind. The original World's Tallest Windmill was toppled in a windstorm (ironic, isn't it?) in 1926, and the replica was built in Littlefield in 1969. I don't know, I felt kind of let down by this news. Kind of like finding out Dolly Parton wears a padded bra. You get yourself all set up to see something humongous and then it turns out the real thing isn't real after all, it's just a replica. Life as a journalist on the open road isn't all fun and games, I'll tell you.

Oklahoma Is OK

We hit the road again Monday morning and followed Highway 385 north to Interstate 40, where we turned east and made tracks for Oklahoma. But before we could finish our stay in Texas, I had one more stop to make.

The Cadillac Ranch isn't really a ranch at all, it's a collection of vintage Cadillac automobiles that a man named Stanley Marsh sunk nose-first into the dirt of the Texas Panhandle just west of Amarillo as an art statement. Over the years, the oddball sculpture

Meandering Down The Highway

has become a Route 66 icon, and though the Interstate has swallowed much of the old road, its spirit lives on in dedicated road warriors such as yours truly. There was no way I was going to pass the Cadillac Ranch without stopping.

The collection of cars is on the south side of the highway just west of exit 62 and a frontage road takes you past it. We pulled over, walked through the gate and there they were in all their graffiti-splattered splendor, those ancient Caddys that have become a symbol of our automotive age. Marsh encourages people to adorn the cars with graffiti as a statement of their passing, and every year the latest messages on the cars are painted over so new visitors can start all over again. I didn't leave my message to the world, but I took several photos and, duty fulfilled, we returned to our motorhome. Miss Terry doesn't always understand why such oddball traditions are so important to me, but she lets me drag her along to all sorts of strange places like this and never complains. Life is good.

Just outside of Groom, Texas, we came across a sign telling us we were about to see the Largest Cross in the Western Hemisphere, and sure enough pretty soon there it was, a huge white cross reaching into the prairie sky. We would have stopped, but once you've seen the replica of the World's Tallest Windmill, other things seem pale in comparison.

Soon Texas was behind us and we found ourselves bouncing over a rough section of highway in Oklahoma. We stopped at the state Welcome Center and loaded up on brochures, then headed for Oklahoma City and Rockwell RV Park.

I need to learn to listen to my wife. Terry had called ahead to confirm that Rockwell RV Park had space available, and that they were a Coast to Coast Good Neighbor Park. We arrived about 7:30 p.m., and driving in passed several trailers that seemed to be long-term units, many with construction type pickups parked in front. Two or three good old boys stood around drinking and

Meandering Down The Highway

spitting, but seemed friendly enough. Terry said she wasn't too impressed with the place, though it had big pull through spaces and lots of things to offer, such as a laundry, cable TV and pool. We had planned to stay two or three days, but decided to stay overnight and see what the morning brought. Since the office was closed when we arrived, the next morning I went in to register. The lady at the desk had obviously left her personality in her other clothes or something, because she was about as friendly as my ex-wife's attorney. She wouldn't honor the Good Neighbor discount from Coast to Coast, wouldn't allow me to leave any sample copies of the *Gypsy Journal* for the other guests, and made it very clear to me that the sooner I left, the sooner she could get back to the talk show she was watching on television. We left, and will find someplace else to stay in the future.

Traffic was light in Oklahoma City, and soon we were on the Turner Turnpike heading toward Tulsa. It cost us $11 to drive 90 miles on the turnpike, which offended the Scrooge in me. A short distance outside of Tulsa we came upon Claremore, the hometown of cowboy philosopher Will Rogers, who used his dry wit and an amazing skill with rope tricks to shape the opinions of the nation back before television brought us situation comedies, Barbara Walters, and MTV. Claremore has a beautiful museum honoring Will Rogers, and just a few miles down the road you can actually park your RV overnight on the farm Rogers grew up on for a very low donation, something like $10. You owe it to yourself to visit the Will Rogers Center in Claremore, but plan on spending several hours to really see it. I guarantee that if you weren't a Will Rogers fan before your visit, you will be by the time you leave.

Winding Our Way Through The Ozarks

Still sniveling about having to pay turnpike tolls, I decided to cheat the state of Oklahoma out of a few dollars by taking secondary roads into Missouri. It seemed like a good idea at the

Meandering Down The Highway

time. Hindsight should have taught me by now that when I have one of these flashes of brilliance, the best thing to do would be to put on my sunglasses and sit down until it passes. Highway 20 out of Claremore started out narrow and winding, widened to a four lane divided roadway for a handful of miles, then diminished back down to a two lane road again. From there it got worse, sharp turns, narrow lanes, and our speed dropped to about 25 miles an hour.

We crossed into Arkansas and came to Bentonville. Noticing a huge parking lot filled with cars, I asked Miss Terry what employer in such a small town could use so many people. About then we spotted the sign for Wal-Mart's World Headquarters. Representing all of us RVers who spend nights at Camp Wal-Mart when we're on the road, we genuflected and continued on our way.

According to Rand McNally we were about 90 miles from our intended destination, Branson, Missouri. If I had an idea what a rough 90 miles it was going to be, I know we would have thought again. Highway 62 took us out of Bentonville past the Pea Ridge Civil War battlefield, and soon we hooked up with Highway 86 and climbed into the Ozarks toward Eureka Springs. The highway soon had us longing for the road we had been complaining about back in Oklahoma. It's a beautiful drive through some of the prettiest countryside we have ever seen, but it's all uphill and downhill, and full of curves marked 15 and 20 miles per hour. There were almost no places to pull over to allow traffic behind us to pass, and soon a long line of cars was trailing us as we rocked around curves and struggled up short, steep hills. I would have liked to have seen more of the countryside, but the narrow highway reduced my sightseeing to furtive glances out across the valleys before I turned my attention back to the highway. RV author and columnist Charlene "Charlie" Minshall wrote me an e-mail later saying she was sure most of the roads in

Meandering Down The Highway

the Ozarks were laid out by a snake, and I have to agree. They were as crooked as my ex-wife's lawyer. It took us three hours to negotiate the 90 miles from Bentonville to Branson, and to add to the fun, our brakes began to fade on the constant hills and sharp turns. By the time we arrived in Branson, I was ready to park it for a few days.

Big Fun In Branson

We've always wanted to visit Branson, and it was everything we had hoped for and more. Someone once described the place to me as a redneck Las Vegas minus the gambling. There's probably some truth to that statement, but if you want entertainment, this is the place to be.

Many people think of Branson as being all about country music, and there are definitely plenty of banjos and steel guitars twanging all over the place, but Branson is much more than that. There are dozens of shows to suit every taste, from country, to bluegrass, to old rock and roll, to comedy. Besides all the music offerings, there is the Silver Dollar City theme park, several amusement parks, and some of the best fishing you can find anywhere. You would have to work at it not to have a good time in Branson. And there are RV parks everywhere, ranging from very fancy to very basic.

We stayed at the Escapees Club Turkey Creek RV Village in Hollister, just a couple of miles from Branson. The park is nice, the location is great, and the staff very friendly. About the only thing wrong with it was that they don't have a Social Hour every afternoon like most Escapees parks do. Apparently everyone is off fishing and seeing shows and having fun, so the Social Hour never works out. That's a disappointment, since one of the things we really appreciate at an Escapees park is the chance to meet our fellow club members and visit with them. It really adds to the feeling of kinship we have with other Escapees. The town of Hollister was built around an English theme, with one street

Meandering Down The Highway

designed as a typical street in an English village, lined with small antique shops and restaurants.

Branson has done a lot to ease traffic congestion with the implementation of three bypass routes, the Red, Blue, and Yellow Routes. But Highway 78, Branson's version of the "Strip" is a bumper to bumper, stop and go nightmare most of the time. One thing that struck us most about Branson is how friendly everyone is, from workers in the stores and restaurants to people in the many campgrounds we visited. In so many resort areas the locals seem to get jaded with the tourists and are a little less then outgoing. Not so in Branson. Everyone we met there went out of their way to be friendly and make us feel welcome. While we were in Branson we stopped at a shop where Miss Terry introduced me to funnel cakes, a decadent concoction of strawberries, ice cream, whipped cream all piled into a warm crisp, yet tender funnel cake and topped with a small waffle cone. I could feel my waistline expand as I ate it. We spent a week in Branson and it wasn't enough. This is one location we'll be returning to many times in our travels.

The Secret That Is Missouri

How come no one ever told me about Missouri? My friend and fellow Escapee John Marschalk is from Missouri, and he's always telling me where to go. So how come he never told me to go to Missouri? All I knew about the state was that Jesse James hung out in the caves here, there's a big arch in St. Louis, old Route 66 crossed the state, and one of the two Kansas Cities is here. What I never knew was how pretty Missouri is, or how friendly the people are just about everywhere you go.

When we left Branson we stopped for gasoline in Springfield, wandered through Bass Pro Shops for a couple of hours, then hooked up with Interstate 44, traveling east. We passed miles of rolling farmland, everything as green as could be, and stopped for the night at Merameo Valley RV Camp Resort, a

Meandering Down The Highway

Coast to Coast park near Cuba, Missouri. The park was huge, with all sorts of amenities and a nice fishing lake.

The weatherman was predicting strong thunderstorms, but except for a nice breeze, the night was calm and we were on the road early the next morning. I took a wrong turn coming out of the RV park and we found ourselves on a narrow country road, searching for a place to turn our big rig around. After a few miles we spotted a church with a parking lot just large enough to make a u-turn in, and we were finally headed back in the right direction.

Our first stop of the day was the famous Meramec Caverns, which turned out to be a disappointment. The road into the Caverns is narrow and has a couple of rather steep hills, but if you take your time and give oncoming traffic as much room as you can, it's no real problem. The Caverns have a big parking lot, with lots of room to park any size rig, as well as a campground. One thing that impressed us was a sign on the entrance door to the Caverns warning that pets shouldn't be locked up in hot cars, and offering free kennel services.

Meramec Caverns is a tourist trap obviously, what with it's large gift shop and fudge stand and such, but we couldn't get anyone in management to give us a couple of minutes to get some background information to help with our story. After being told the manager was on a personal phone call and to wait a few minutes that stretched to well over half an hour, we decided to leave and find something else to write about. Back at the Interstate, we wanted to stop at the Antique Toy Museum in Stanton to see their huge collection of collectable toys dating back from the turn of the century (that would be the 20th Century, for all you Y2K freaks) to the 1960s. But the museum was closed, as was the Jesse James Wax Museum next door. Some days you just can't find any place to write about.

Driving through Missouri, I was thinking about all of my friends in our classic car club back in Arizona. It seems like every

Meandering Down The Highway

farmhouse and roadside business we passed had some old car or truck from the 1940s through 1960s for sale, most of which would make excellent restoration projects.

Our next stop was frontiersman Daniel Boone's home, near Defiance, Missouri. Most people think of Kentucky when they think of Daniel Boone, but the frontiersman actually lived out the last seventeen years of his life on a beautiful farm in frontier Missouri. While the people at Meramec Caverns couldn't be bothered with us, the folks at the Historic Daniel Boone Home and Boonesfield Village went out of their way to be accommodating, giving us a guided tour of the home and several period buildings that have been moved onto the property. When I was a kid, Daniel Boone was one of my biggest heroes. Not the Hollywood version we saw on screen, but the true frontiersman who helped open the wild country that would become Kentucky and Tennessee. To stand in Boone's home, to touch the woodwork that he hand-crafted himself, to see the actual bed he slept (and died) in, was a moving experience. The drive in to Boone's home is through beautiful farm land over narrow country lanes which had us wondering if our RV could squeeze past an oncoming farm truck if we met up with one (we didn't), but it was well worth the effort.

Following directions we got at Daniel Boone's home, we drove several miles to a small hilltop cemetery where he and his wife Rebecca were buried after she died in 1813 and Boone passed away in 1820. There was a very small pullout across the road from the cemetery that we just managed to sneak our big rig in to. You will find a complete feature on Daniel Boone's home and the mystery surrounding his final resting place in this issue.

Mark Twain Country

We arrived at Tievoli Hills Resort near Clarksville, Missouri late in the afternoon and settled in for a few days to explore Hannibal, home of Mark Twain and his fictional characters Tom

Meandering Down The Highway

Sawyer and Huck Finn and their adventures on the Mississippi River.

Clarksville is the winter nesting place to hundreds of bald eagles, and visitors from all over the world come to watch the great birds as they fish in the Mississippi River and nest in the nearby hills. The Clarksville Eagle Center, a satellite educational facility of the World Bird Sanctuary in St. Louis, gives visitors the chance to view the eagles close up and learn more about wildlife.

At the Eagle Center you can take part in programs on eagles and other raptors, learn about ecology, touch a snake and even experience the sound of hissing cockroaches. (Where else but the *Gypsy Journal* would you learn about such opportunities?) Admission to the Clarksville Eagle Center is free, and they are open seven days a week. For more information, you can call them at (573)242-3132.

Clarksville is about 45 miles south of Hannibal, but the drive along the Mississippi is very pretty and there are frequent pullouts where you can stop to watch the river, see tugboats pushing barges down the river, and just drink in the scenery. A few miles north of Clarksville we came to Louisiana, a small river town that has seen better days. Most of the buildings in the downtown area are either empty or occupied with rundown looking second hand stores. But the architecture of the town is just wonderful. There are dozens of beautiful old Victorian homes, many of which have been restored and turned into bed and breakfast operations. There is also a river front park that makes a great place for a picnic, and all of the people we met were very friendly.

We weren't surprised to see that Hannibal lives and breathes on tourism, but we were delighted by the fact that everyone was so warm and outgoing. Again, as in Branson, we didn't see the impersonal attitudes that people in so many tourist areas seem to have. Linda Gottman and her staff at the Visitors Bureau and Ila

Meandering Down The Highway

Woolen at the Mark Twain Boyhood Home and Museum went out of their way to make us feel welcome and to help us in every way they could to make our visit more enjoyable. There are all sorts of family activities going on all year long, so no matter when you visit Hannibal, you'll have fun.

Looking back, our only regret about our visit to Hannibal was that we didn't stay in one of the campgrounds there, instead of down in Clarksville. The drive back and forth was pretty, but took up a lot of time every day. If we hadn't already pre-paid at Tievoli Hills, we would have parked the rig in Hannibal. There are several RV parks in Hannibal, including Mark Twain Cave Campgrounds and Bayview Camper's Park, both of which impressed us. We got a nice surprise when we stopped at Mark Twain Cave Campgrounds to drop off a bundle of sample copies of the *Gypsy Journal*. Subscribers Bill and Gloria Eversole were working at the campgrounds for the season and we had a chance to get acquainted. At Bayview Camper's Park, the owner and I spent an hour or so visiting and I came away with a new friend. We'll be returning to Hannibal again, one trip wasn't nearly enough, and we'll stay in town next time.

Mark Twain Lake, maybe a half hour drive from Hannibal, is 18,600 surface acres of sparkling water, offering fishing, hiking, boating, and several campgrounds. The lake is surrounded by over 38,000 acres of land managed by the Corps of Engineers, so there is plenty of room to play in. They routinely pull some large bass and crappie from the lake, as well as catfish topping forty pounds, so if you're a fisherman, this is the place to be. The Landing is a water fun park and campground that is popular with families and the place was busy when we visited.

As this issue wraps up, we find ourselves still enjoying the hospitality of Missouri, and taking some time to get everything rearranged in the RV from having to unload it for its trip to the factory. It's amazing the things we've discovered we didn't know

Meandering Down The Highway

we still owned. Now we have to decide if it's worth hauling them around any more after not using them for the last year. We find that the more we travel, the less we need to own. That's one of the best things about life on the open road, freedom from the "stuff" so many people find themselves tied down with.

From here, we'll venture into Illinois and Indiana, spend some time around my old home town of Toledo, Ohio, and then wander up to Michigan, maybe cross the Upper Peninsula into Wisconsin and see what adventures await us there.

We never worry about finding something interesting to visit and write about as we travel. The hard part is trying to find enough hours in the day to do everything we want to do, yet still enjoy our free time too. It's a tough life seeing new things every day, meeting new people, and exploring this great land of ours. Sometimes we envy all those folks stuck behind a desk somewhere knowing they'll be doing the same thing tomorrow and the next day and the next for the next twenty or thirty years. (And if you believe that, I met a fellow in Missouri that has a bridge to sell you!) Until next time, hope to see you in our travels.

Meandering Down The Highway

Epilogue

Life is an continuously evolving adventure. In the months following the completion of this book we saw several changes . Sometimes as we cruise down the highway of life, we suddenly hit a speed bump and the bottom drops out of our world. We hit such a speed bump while visiting family in Traverse City, Michigan on the night of Thursday, September 28, 2000. Terry had been having abdominal pain for some time, and about 10 p.m. that night she started hemorrhaging. By the time I got her to the emergency room, she had lost about two-thirds of her body's blood supply and was in serious trouble. The ER staff swarmed around her, and after some touch and go, were able to staunch the bleeding. Then they began to look for the cause. I felt like someone had hit me with a sledgehammer when the doctor told me it was advanced cervical cancer.

Cancer. No, things like that happen to other people, not to us. Not to my beautiful, wonderful wife. Not to my best friend. We had just found each other three years before. We had just started our new life on the road. There had to be a mistake. There was no mistake.

I don't believe anyone has ever received the love and support Miss Terry and I did in the days following her diagnosis. We were parked in my cousin Terry Cook's driveway, and he and his wife Peggy let us know we were welcome to stay for as long as we needed. I contacted family and close friends, and immediately the word spread, and letters and calls started coming in. Our families,

Meandering Down The Highway

our friends back in our hometown in Arizona, and the many RVing friends we have made during our time on the road let us know we were not alone.

RVing friends offered to change their travel plans and come to Traverse City to be with us in our time of need. Several offered to donate blood for Terry, including some RVers we didn't know, but who had heard of her illness. Terry's parents, Pete and Bess Weber, fulltimers themselves, were in Utah when they got the news, and wanted to drive across the country to be by her side. Meanwhile, the wonderful staff at Munson Memorial Medical Center in Traverse City embraced us. Several nurses who have survived cancer themselves took the time to talk to Terry on their own time and reassure her. One nurse went so far as to offer us the use of her property to park our RV on for the duration of Terry's treatment.

Once Terry was stabilized, we talked about seeking treatment somewhere else. Living in an RV means you can go wherever you want or need to. It was early October, and cold weather was just around the corner. Treatment would take about eight weeks. Would we be better off heading for warmer country? We decided we were very comfortable with, and had a tremendous amount of confidence in, the staff at Munson and the adjacent Biederman Cancer Center, and that we would stay here for the radiation/chemotherapy regime.

I have known some brave people in my life. True heroes. Soldiers who stood their ground in the face of overwhelming odds, while everybody around them turned and ran. Police officers who took on the dirty, dangerous jobs the rest of society doesn't want to deal with. But never in my time on this earth have I seen anyone with the courage of my beloved wife as she faced this terrible challenge. The first words out of Terry's lips after hearing her diagnosis were "I'm going to beat this. We've got too much left to do." With that steadfast courage, and with the grace

Meandering Down The Highway

and poise with which she lives every other aspect of her life, Miss Terry set her goal on a complete recovery.

It was the roughest road we've ever traveled together. Never have I felt so impotent as I did having to watch my darling suffer through the rigors of radiation and chemotherapy, the nausea, the pain, the weight loss, and not being able to do anything to help her. More than once I begged God to take me if one of us had to go. But the marvels of modern medicine and the power of prayer combined to bring us through our rough journey, and today the doctors tell Miss Terry the cancer is gone. She is growing stronger every day, and the worst is behind us. So many people were there for us - family, friends, readers, people we met in our travels. We appreciate and love all of you for helping us through our nightmare.

We recently purchased an MCI bus and are in the process of converting it to replace the Motorhome From Hell. Every mail delivery brings more subscriptions as the *Gypsy Journal's* readership grows. At every RV rally we attend, at every campground we stop to spend the night, and at every small town museum and historical site we visit, we meet interesting people and make new friends.

We continue our meandering together, never knowing what adventures await us down the road and around the next bend. Life is wonderful.

Meandering Down The Highway

Come Along For The Ride!

The adventure continues, and you can be a part of it! Subscribe to the *Gypsy Journal* today and continue to ride along with our two modern day ramblers as they explore America's highways and back roads, introducing you to small town museums, little known attractions, historical sites, and the weird, wacky, and wonderful people they meet along the way. Just $15 for one year or $25 for two years brings you all the fun! (Canadian subscriptions, please add $5) All subscriptions delivered by first class mail to insure forwarding for our traveling readers.

More Great Reading From The Gypsy Journal!

Gypsy Journal's Guide to Free Campgrounds & Overnight Parking Spots - Save hundreds of dollars every year with our list of over 500 free and low cost campgrounds from coast to coast! City and county parks, public lands, RV friendly businesses, and commercial locations where you can park for free or just a few dollars. Hundreds of RVers are saving money every day with this fantastic information. Available in printed booklet or on 3.5 PC disk formatted for Windows. Just $8.95, it pays for itself the first time you use it!

RVers Guide to Fairgrounds Camping - Looking for a safe, inexpensive place to spend a few days, but the area you are visiting does not allow dry camping in the local Wally World parking lot? Are the local RV parks full? Learn how you can discover new camping opportunities and save money by camping at fairgrounds nationwide. Our booklet lists over 250 fairgrounds that offer RV camping nationwide, with rates, telephone numbers and

Meandering Down The Highway

e-mail addresses for most. Just $7.50, a great bargain for RVers!

RVers Guide to Modem Friendly Truck Stops - Get your e-mail on the road! Computers have become an essential tool for modern RVers. Internet access on the road allows RVers to do banking, pay bills online, and keep in touch with family and friends from the road. Many truck stops around the country now have modem hookups and allow RVers to plug in and get online. We have assembled a list of over 200 truck stops across the country that provide modem access. A valuable tool when you are on the road! Just $6.95.

Work Your Way Across The USA - Can you really make enough money to travel fulltime in an RV? Nick Russell says yes! The author of *Meandering Down The Highway* has taught classes and conducted seminars on working on the road at RV rallies across the country. Now he brings this valuable information to you in a new book packed with ideas for jobs and small businesses that can help make your dream of fulltiming come true! Whether you only need to make a few dollars a month to supplement your retirement, or you need a fulltime income, this is the book that will show you how! Only $12.95, plus $3.50 shipping.

To order subscriptions, books, or booklets, send payment to Gypsy Journal, 1400 Colorado, Suite C-16, Boulder City, Nevada 89005 or log onto www.paypal.com and make payment to gypsyjrnl@aol.com. Visit our website at www.gypsyjournal.net. or e-mail Nick Russell at editor@gypsyjournal.net.

Printed in the United States
43372LVS00002B/58-63